Soul Business

A Search for God at Work in Our Work

By

Paul Bruno and Laura Capp

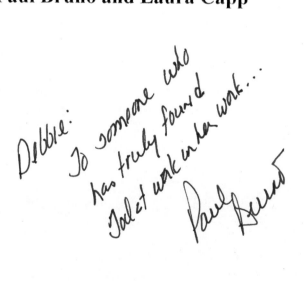

Debbie: To someone who has truly found God at work in her work...

Paul Bruno

ISBN: 1-4033-8067-8 (e-book)
ISBN: 1-4033-8068-6 (Paperback)

Library of Congress Control Number: 2002094875

This book is printed on acid free paper.

Printed in the United States of America
Bloomington, IN

1stBooks rev. 02/12/03

Dedication

To my lovely wife, Susie,
my steadfast example of a person
who humbly seeks and gracefully finds God at work in
her work
and life each day.

Paul

For Jenna,
the daughter of my dreams
and my greatest blessing.

Laura (*Mom*)

Acknowledgements

We have been blessed with many cheerleaders in the creation of this book. Some have served as sources of inspiration; others have given their thoughtful consideration and feedback to our earlier drafts; and still more have assisted us in the final production of *Soul Business*. We would like to acknowledge the contribution of all of these friends and colleagues for their caring support and professionalism.

Mary Lou Andrews for the final preparation of our manuscript

Gary Martin for his spectacular cover art

Amy Barnes at 1st Books Library

Our reviewers and gentle critics:

Philip F. Deaver
Tom and Maureen Kramlinger
Janice Brewi, c.s.j.
Anne Brennan, c.s.j.
Louise Franklin-Sheehy
The Very Reverend and Mrs. C. Joseph Sitts
Barbara Adler
Cheryl Hanson
Annette Kelly

Phyllis Layman
Kathy Hurley
Cynthia Hasenau
Beth Jensen
Jean Wilkinson
Linda Roberts
Tim and Barb Trombitas
Pam Stewart

Others who helped, encouraged, and inspired us:

Tom Barry
Cynthia and Jessamyn Baker
Terry DeLaPorte & DeLaPorte Associates
The Reverend Mark Rivera
Bill Paynter
Beverly Paulk
Michael and Katherine Bruno
Kim Bruno and Matt Bauer
Katharine Boyer
Catherine Leister
Paulette Geller
Cathy Lieblich
Paul Schmid, D.O.
Ray Capp
Esther Capp

Table of Contents

Part One

First Thoughts

> **"Put your ear down next to your soul
> and listen hard."**
> Anne Sexton

We didn't set out to write a religious book, but the more we talked to each other and to others, we discovered God's handprint everywhere we turned. It wasn't an obtrusive or authoritarian hand—no wagging a finger at you or patting you condescendingly on the head. It was a handprint so subtle that we might have missed it but for the fact that no other plausible explanation for certain turns of events could explain it away. We're tough-minded business people, for heaven's sake; was God really lurking behind the water cooler?

Still, we, and others we spoke with, kept coming up empty-handed when it came to understanding the source of the inner voice, the soulful yearning, the quest for something more. We are Christians, but we think we've written a book that has meaning for anyone who believes in a Higher Power, a Supreme Being. Our goal is not to evangelize, but to tell our stories and share our learning. If we do it well, our words will move you and become a set of lenses that enable you to see inside to your sacred place—and in so doing, see the handprint of the Mighty One.

Who We Are

We are the most unlikely of compatriots. Paul is a

down-to-his-bones sales guy with a distinguished career at a major high tech corporation and later, a sales director for a large training company. He's been married to the same woman, herself an Episcopal deacon, for over 30 years. They have two grown children and two beloved Golden Retrievers. Laura is a single mom who started out as a teacher and eventually led the consulting services team of the same training company. That is where we met, but it wasn't until years later—when we had both left that firm to start independent businesses of our own—that we found ourselves fellow travelers down the same rocky path.

While we had known each other for nine years and had done some work together on occasion, our respective assignments gave us little need to collaborate. After Paul left the company, we kept in touch, sharing excitement over his new "Refocus" business. When, a year or so later, Laura left the company, we often discussed practical matters like registering a company name, finding an insurance agent, and investing 401-K rollover funds. We still didn't foresee that the Spirit would draw us into a working friendship—and in such an unpredictable way.

Paul had been calling on a local client, a training manager in a major real estate development corporation. The client, Randy, was struggling with a variety of tough issues—trying to get employees to accept recent changes, trying to get teams to take ownership of process improvements. Paul thrived on helping organizations deal with these change management issues, and Randy encouraged Paul to fashion his ideas into a training program. Despite his sound approach, Paul admitted he was not an instructional designer. He would need help creating a training program that would be engaging and meaningful for Randy's staff.

At the same time that Paul and Randy were having these discussions, Laura was completing her last official task for her former employer—pilot testing a new training program. Randy and his staff were among those who participated in the daylong event, and Randy was impressed with the work Laura had done. Knowing Laura was about to strike out on her own, Randy suggested that we team up to work on the program Paul had proposed. Randy seemed emphatic that we had just the right combination of skills, and that, working together, we could create something memorable. Neither of us had considered the possibility of our working together but, needing Randy's business, we were willing to give it a try.

We completed that project for Randy, and in the process, developed a mutual respect and a comfortable working arrangement for both of us. We went on to tackle other projects together when the right opportunities arose, but we meet regularly to support each other, even when our businesses take us in different directions. Over corned beef and potato salad, we have often reflected on the unexpected way our paths were brought together by the Spirit guiding a client to make the connection that we didn't see.

Becoming sole proprietors, struggling to make it on our own, led us to reconnect for support and encouragement. We began with monthly pep rallies at a local restaurant. In those once-a-month luncheons we shared the state of our businesses and the state of our souls. We found, in each other, a person who was experiencing similar feelings, thinking similar thoughts, and trying to make it on his/her own. We didn't offer each other pat advice from the latest popular business books; instead we found ourselves relying on faith-based examples to characterize the confusion and discouragement we often felt. One month we would feel that we had thrown the seeds of ideas and proposals onto rocks, where they would never flourish. The next month we would rejoice, because the checks had finally come in like manna from heaven. We were struggling together and learning together, and we might have a message that connects with you.

What we found is that the business landscape is a treacherous place, especially for the lone entrepreneur; surviving it, succeeding in it made believers out of us. It made us stop and take notice of all that we believe and all that we are. Those that make it in small business have faith—not only in themselves, but in something greater than themselves. With each other's help, each of us learned to follow our own internal compass for direction, rather than somebody else's barometer of success. We discovered that the business we're in is *soul business*.

Is This Book for You?

You may be wondering if this book is for you, if it is worth your time to read it. We can tell you what we are not. We do not have between us an MBA, a PhD or even a divinity degree. Our conclusions are not based on research or years of academic study. We do not posit any business theories, theological concepts, or psychological constructs. We can also tell you who we are—school-of-hard-knocks business people with a commitment to spiritual growth. Our experiences are uniquely personal and, as we have come to learn, surprisingly common.

While entrepreneurship has opened our eyes and focused our minds on the faith-based journey, we recognize that our experiences and the Twelve Faith-Based Qualities are not limited to entrepreneurs. As we have shared our ideas with colleagues and friends, we have been encouraged about how our themes resonate with people working in a variety of circumstances. So, while being an entrepreneur lends urgency to these issues, the substance of our experience is common to many in the world of work today.

If you are questioning the purpose of the work you do or reminiscing about career roads not taken, this book may be for you. If your chosen career seems to feel too tight or too small lately, you may want to read on. If you are struggling to blend your public image with your private yearnings for more meaningful work, we might have words you need to hear. You may be contemplating starting your own business or rethinking how you want to spend the second half of your life. You may be in the throes of reacting to a major life change or redefining what is important to you and how you want to behave differently on a day-to-day basis. Wherever you are in life, but especially if you are experiencing a middle-aged transition, you might view our stories as a catalyst to examining your own.

How This Book Is Organized

In Part One of *Soul Business* we tell our stories, beginning with the personal struggles that led up to our mutual decisions to take the leap from full time employment to independent consulting. We share the lessons we have learned, and those we keep relearning—lessons about professional and personal balance, commitment and risk. We share the faith that has kept us growing and searching together as entrepreneurs. Part One concludes with a set of reflections, questions you may want to wrestle with yourself or with a group of trusted friends and colleagues.

In Part Two, we present the Twelve Faith-Based Qualities that we believe underlie the entrepreneurial, indeed, the life journey. We explain the significance of these Qualities and how you can recognize and develop them. We leave you with a set of twelve meditations, one for each month and each faith-based quality, and give you the opportunity to reflect on these Qualities in your own business and life.

Soul Business began to emerge as we shared our journals month to month. We didn't set a goal to define Twelve Faith-Based Qualities; they emerged out of our shared experiences. We didn't attempt to devise a road map for linking work and faith, but over time it was revealed. Like many of you, we're still not sure where we're headed, but we have often sensed God at work in our work of writing this book, a vehicle for His timeless values. We hope that the time you spend reading our reflections will cause you to reflect and to spend some time on your own soul business.

Paul Bruno   Laura Capp
Longwood, FL   Oviedo, FL

Reflections

- *What people have entered your life as "unlikely compatriots"? Were you open to establishing a relationship with someone you didn't expect? What opportunities did you miss by prejudging others or simply lacking awareness?*

- *How have others served as conduits in your life and career? Has someone connected you to another you wouldn't have known or wouldn't have chosen to know better? Have you taken time to cultivate bridging relationships that may lead you to the place you need to go?*

- *Do you have at least one person in your life with whom you feel safe speaking honestly and showing your vulnerability? Do you have someone in your life with whom you feel comfortable laughing at yourself? If not, what can you do to develop an existing relationship into one that would nurture your soul?*

- *Do you judge yourself and your success based on external measures, such as bonuses, awards and perks? What is your personal definition of success? At the end of your life, which of your accomplishments will be most satisfying to you?*

- *Have you ever considered the role God plays in the work you do? What God-given talents have contributed to your success? When was the last time you thanked God for these gifts? How could you give God something back as a way of saying thanks?*

I Was Bored to Death: Paul's Story

> *"In order that people may be happy in their work, these three things are needed: They must be fit for it, they must not do too much of it. And they must have a sense of success in it."*
> John Ruskin

I Was Bored To Death: Paul's Story

It was a short and detailed dream. I was on a stage at a local community college and looking out at a graduation audience for the Center for High Tech Training for Individuals with Disabilities, a group I had been volunteering with for some time. I had been introduced by a woman who was wearing a purple dress, "You all know Paul. I'll turn it over to him." Later, as I processed this dream, I realized that the woman "in purple" was my wife of 34 years, Susie. My father too was in the audience, and I could see him clearly to my left as I heard myself say, "I was 48 years old and woke up one morning and realized that I was bored to death."

Some years ago, I was in the process of establishing a call center for another company. We were selling skill-based, computer-scored assessments by telephone. The selling protocol had been designed; the "telesales" scripts had been written; and my daily routine began to feel very mechanical. The challenge of convincing the parent company that our little unit had revenue potential had been overcome. We weren't experiencing any new and creative objections to buying our product. Our targeted markets were clearly defined, and new sales were coming on a daily basis. There weren't any new products on the drawing board. We fell into our daily, weekly, and monthly routines of mailing out product announcements; follow-up sales calling; and attending meetings for the sake of attending meetings. It was time to move on, but move on to what...move on to where?

I wasn't interested in another job or career path inside the company. At long last, I knew that my career and personal growth had plateaued. I saw my children and my wife all moving forward in their lives and their own careers. I felt very much alone, and I resented the people, *including myself*, who had put me on the shelf at 48 years of age. I hadn't taken advantage of my proximity to computers in the company, so I was at best a novice in my understanding of the benefits of the new "information age." I had only myself to blame. Alone, resentful, and critical of myself, I was not happy. This was not a good time in my life.

I sensed that my greatest ally was change and how quickly the world seemed to be changing around me. I also knew that I had to take what I had become at that point--*the good and the not so good*--and get ready to do something more with my life. It was time to acknowledge my dreams and take a leap of faith. When this realization took hold, I began a new chapter in my adulthood and business career. A career door was closing in my life; the corporate work chapters had been written; I had no idea where I was going to go.

My ultimate source of comfort was my family. I could look at Susie, my children, Michael and Kim, and feel that, at least here, off the job, that I had done some things right. They would be there to support me, and this meant that I was free to move on. I had no excuses or reasons to procrastinate. Along the way, I began to reach out for help for the first time in my adult life.

I Took My Son To Lunch and He Named the Company

We were sitting over lunch, and my 23-year-old son, Michael, looked at me and asked, "Now, Dad, just what are you trying to accomplish with this new company?" I thought for a minute and responded, "I'm trying to help people rethink and reshape their motivations for working in their jobs and help them develop a purposeful approach to their work that engages and excites them." Michael thought about my answer and responded, "Well, Dad, it sound like you're going to try to help them refocus."

Inspired, I got up from the table and called my attorney. One hour later *RE*Focus, Inc. was a new company with a purpose statement that read: "Challenging people and organizations to find and chart new routes to success."

A Faith-Based Purpose is Your Touchstone

When you go into business for yourself, you had better

have a purpose for your enterprise that goes beyond just making a lot of money. You can always work for someone else and earn a comfortable living. Regardless of where you find yourself at this point in your life, the fact is that God will continue to provide you with new circumstances that will result in new learning, decisions, and new life directions.

Have you ever taken the time to ask, "Why God? Why now? Why me?" Have you ever taken the time to ponder what God's purpose could be for your work? Have you ever consciously attempted to align your professional goals to what you believe His purpose could be for your career? Laura and I hope that *Soul Business* challenges you to begin asking these questions. We pray that our stories encourage you to open yourself up to these new possibilities.

One of my hopes for you is that our book will help you discover and define God's purpose for your work. Your *faith-based purpose* outlines how you will be serving your fellow man as you live into God's purpose for the remainder of your career. It is your personal work covenant with God. Your purpose serves as a reference point that you can revisit as you evaluate the relevance of your efforts. A belief in the faith-based aspect of your purpose motivates you, keeps you going when you are tempted to seek the easier direction or simply give up.

I've found that when you own the company it's hard to remain objective. A faith-based purpose statement helps me evaluate the courses of action that I need to retain as well as the decisions and behaviors that I need to let go. As a matter of fact, I simply evaluate my performance at the end of the day in terms of my response to my son's original question years ago, "Now, Dad, just what are you trying to accomplish with this company?"

Michael, *RE*Focus is all about…
> *"Challenging people and organizations to find and chart new routes to success."*

The People that God Sends into Our Lives

"As you know, those people were of no consequence."

I tell this story often when I'm completing a presentation. The day was Tuesday, August 20, 1991. My wife, Susie, and I were in Moscow with a 34-member missionary team. It was the second day of the Russian coup, and the "hard-liners" in the Kremlin had placed President Gorbachev and his wife under house arrest while they were vacationing in the Crimea. If the new government had its way, initiatives that were designed to open Soviet markets and improve relations with the West would slow dramatically. The people of the Soviet Union were going to return to a state of government-enforced disciplines and the more comfortable predictability of the overt rule of the Communist Party. On Tuesday morning, it was apparent to the new leadership that the outside world was not reacting positively to the new government or the new direction.

Given all these events, our missionary team was "invited" to the Kremlin for a tour. We boarded a bus and drove into the center of the city. The military presence in the city was pervasive in the form of troops, tanks, and armored personnel carriers. I remember walking between tanks as we were escorted through the perimeter walls of the Kremlin and working hard at convincing myself that we were going to be okay, because we had been invited to "come on down" by this new government.

A woman, who was an official of the Communist Party, met us in a rotunda area. Customer service and interpersonal skills were not her strong points, and it was apparent by her facial expressions, tone of voice, and gestures that she didn't like Americans. Our guide "welcomed" us on behalf of the new government and informed us that we would be touring the Armory, located in the basement of the Kremlin. I liken the Armory to our Smithsonian Institution. The displays centered on the histories of the Russian Czars and their families. The exhibit halls contained valuable artifacts of art, pottery, jewelry, clothing, carriages, and written histories for each family in the succession.

It was in the second room on the tour that Cynthia, a friend and artist, noticed that the paintings hanging on display were unsigned. She asked our guide for an explanation, and the question was ignored. In fact, the question was stonewalled, and we knew that our guide had heard and understood Cynthia's query. A number of us noted the incident and, when we went to the next display area, we accompanied Cynthia when she broke away from the main group to view that room's paintings. As before, there were no signatures on many of these paintings either. This time Cynthia blocked the exit to the next exhibit and challenged our guide, "I know you understand the question. I want to know why those paintings aren't signed!"

The response was chilling. "Those paintings aren't signed, because they were painted by serfs and peasants. As you know, those people were of no consequence." I will never forget the stunned silence and then the reaction. Thirty-four American missionaries forgot where they were and just got angry. The response came from somewhere over my right shoulder, "Well lady with an attitude like that, it doesn't surprise me that you folks can't get any food on your supermarkets' shelves." So ended our tour.

I believe that when people underestimate and diminish the importance of other people, they are ultimately rejecting God's presence in their lives. Some years ago, in Rochester, New York, my wife and I attended a weekly Bible study on Friday evenings. One evening a young woman named Sharon shared her story of being totally bedridden due to a serious problem with her back. She had always been very active, and finding herself totally immobile for months began to wear on her patience. One afternoon, in her frustration and anger, Sharon looked up at God and asked, "And just where are you in all of this?"

His response was simply, "Sharon, I'm in your

presence each day. I'm coming to you through the people who are ministering to you, and I am supporting the people who are taking care of your husband and children." This young woman disclosed how shocked and startled she was when she heard the voice. She found herself looking around the room and calling out. No one was there. Yet Sharon knew that someone was there, and she was humbled by the sense of love and peace that she felt at that moment. Her anger was gone, her fears forgotten. She was now ready to accept her situation, and she went on to fully recover. What if people who come into our lives have been sent by God? What if you are being sent by God into other people's lives?

I Believe That All People are of Consequence: A Business Perspective

In a business setting, technology notwithstanding, I still believe that any positive results enjoyed by a manager reflect the contributions of dedicated and talented employees within the organization. Everyone plays a role in the organization's success. Everyone counts. Everyone is of consequence.

Over the years, I've been fortunate to have a number of assignments that have required me to learn the business and technical portions of the job while concurrently being held accountable for achieving the year's targeted results. In the early stages of these assignments, I found that I was totally dependent on my employees. My orientation process involved getting to know my employees first as individuals;

learning the rudiments of the jobs from my employees' perspectives; and eventually earning the right to communicate my expectations and manage these employees' performance. Over the years, I've learned that there has to be mutual respect and appreciation for each other's knowledge and skills before a manager or an organization will truly be successful.

Recently I was working with employees from a city's public works department in a team building exercise. One of the field workers looked at the department's director and said, "It's not about the money. Sometimes it would be enough if we knew that management really understood what we had gone through to complete this job...and just said thank you."

Sometimes managers forget where they came from and focus on the roles of planning performance, organizing staffs to achieve the goals, and managing that performance after analyzing statistical results. They forget to connect with the people who are doing the work and who are closest to their customers. *They forget the people of consequence within their organizations.*

I Believe That All People Are of Consequence: A Family Perspective

Years ago, my daughter, Kim, was venturing off to college. It was the night before, and I was lying in bed planning our next day. We had packed the cars for the trip with the gear that Kim felt was *absolutely* necessary to survive her first year in a college dormitory. Our son, Michael, was already out on his own and had just completed his first year at the University of Central Florida. Susie and I were on the verge of a new life chapter, the "empty-nest syndrome."

The light in the family room went out; Kim was going to bed. I still remember the rush of emotion that hit me. The words that I remembered saying when I first saw my newborn son, "Our lives will never be the same," came back at that moment. The childhood years were gone forever. Our lives were entering a new chapter. Our lives would never be the same. At that moment I realized how much I was going to miss the children. I began to silently cry, and I looked at my wife and found that she was crying too.

With all the jobs, the homes, the travel, and the pressures, I suddenly wondered if I had fully enjoyed and appreciated our times together as a family. At this point, I realized that there was no going back, no second chances. Had I done the best job as a father and a husband, or had I oftentimes been more engrossed with work or other concerns? There always seemed to be something competing for my attention and participation with my family. These were tough questions to be asking myself on that evening years ago. I realized that Kim and Mike would always have their parents; however at this point in their lives, our parental nurturing and mentoring roles were changing. They were essentially young adults and striking out on their own.

Wherever you are in your career journey, don't forget that *people of consequence in your life start with your family.* They are more important than the money, the titles, the esteem boosting perks, the all-consuming business issues, or the upcoming opportunities. As I've worked at developing my new business, I've come to realize how grateful I am for my immediate family. This perspective and appreciation extends out to our parents and brothers and sisters and now their children. As I've journeyed out on my own, I've now come to realize how loyal and supportive this entire family has been in my career journey. They have listened and advised me on job and career decisions. They have always been there. In short, they have always made me feel of consequence, and this knowledge has sustained me in the good and the bad times.

I Believe That All People are of Consequence: A Community Perspective

When I left the Xerox Corporation, I tasted my first experience of working for a small company and working on my own. Living in Rochester, New York, I signed on to open a one-man office and represent a company headquartered in Santa Rosa, California. I sold a time and life-planning system, and I represented the company from upstate New York/New England to Washington DC.

It didn't take long to set up the new routines of mailing out introductory letters and following these letters up with sales presentations and introductory life-planning training seminars. At first, I enjoyed the freedom to set up my own work plans and schedules. I found that I didn't have a problem opening the office in the upstairs bedroom at 8:00 AM and working my sales calls until 5:00 PM. I was going to be successful on my own terms. I was doing it my way!

About three months into the new routines, I began to feel that something wasn't quite right. I began to realize that something was missing; that I wasn't happy; that my daily contacts with other people were limited mostly to sales calls, sales presentations, and training seminars. I was totally focused on the work, and my scope of contacts with other people was extremely limited. I was talking to a friend who was a general manager with a major insurance company. He had a number of his sales reps working out of their homes as well, and he gave me some advice that I would like to pass on. He said, "Paul, when you work alone, *the solitude works on you.* You need to get out and connect with people in settings other than the work itself."

Over the years, I've found that there are life lessons to be learned from people of consequence who are out there in our communities. Volunteering and working in a thrift shop will teach one about the simple dignity of budgeting and exchanging hard earned coins for used and functional clothing. Working with individuals with disabilities will teach one about the courage needed to face a debilitating life circumstance and then move on to survive productively. Serving as a missionary will teach one about the yearning for

Christ's promise that exists in the far reaches of an embattled world. I believe that every 50+ adult who is physically able should make a conscious decision to serve others. There are people in the world who need and will appreciate our life experiences, and we need to continue learning and gaining new perspectives from their life experiences. Our new teachers in the second halves of our lives are truly people of consequence.

Acknowledging the Source of Your Life's Purpose: Significant People and Your Passion

When I was growing up I can remember a ballad sung by the late Peggy Lee entitled, *Is That All There Is?* As she sang each stanza that described her significant life events, she would end her reminiscing with the phrase, "Is that all there is?" I believe that many of us reach a point in our lives where we look at our material acquisitions and our career accomplishments and begin to ask ourselves the same question.

One evening Susie and I were reviewing the acquisitions and accomplishments in our lives, and my wife paused, looked me in the eye, and said, "Paul, we have so much more to be thankful for. We have wonderful memories!" *Soul Business* is about encouraging you to revisit and rediscover the source of enduring memories in your life. Laura and I hope that our formation stories encourage you to begin a discovery process that enables you to find the ultimate source of your hope, your energy, and the resilience that has driven you forward on life's journey.

My goal for you is that, after you finish our book, you would respond to the question, "Is that all there is?" with a resounding...Look Again!

Reflections

- *Have you experienced a plateau in your career, a time when you were stuck in a rut? What was your response—wallow in self-pity, numb yourself to the day-to-day drudgery? What did you do or could you do to shake things up or find a better situation?*

- *Have you identified God's purpose in your work? What infuses your work with meaning, so that it is both satisfying to you and fills a need for others? How aligned are your career goals with what you believe to be God's purpose for your life?*

- *When was the last time you found yourself in a situation that offended your sense of justice and moral principles? Did you speak up against the injustice? Did you take action to right the wrong in some way? If you had it to do over, would you do anything differently?*

- *If you have people working for you, how do you show them that they are "people of consequence"? What do you do to earn their respect and the right to manage their endeavors? How do you let them know you value their expertise and contribution?*

- *Is there any doubt in the minds of your family members that you love them? Are you sure? Wherever you may be, never let the lights go out without letting your loved ones know how important they are to you. What nighttime ritual can you establish to do this?*

- *Are you getting lost in your work, isolated from the community around you? Have you taken time to consider who might need the very skills and experience you possess? Set a goal to get connected with a charitable organization or cause that needs you and, perhaps, has something to teach you*

Unraveling the Golf Ball: Laura's Story

> *"My business is not to remake myself,*
> *but to make the absolute best of what God made."*
> Robert Browning

Unraveling the Golf Ball

Things began to crumble for me about two years before I actually left the organization. Already the seeds of discontent were sprouting, but I didn't want to see them. I started seeing a therapist, who later became a trusted friend. When we first met, Clara listened intently to my litany of complaints—I wasn't getting the respect I felt I deserved; I wasn't getting the promotion I felt I earned. In those days I was exhausted from carrying my self-appointed load at the office and from barely managing my overwhelming responsibilities at home. I wasn't happy anywhere; my soul was starving. Clara focused intently on me and said words I will always remember, "Maybe the Universe is sending you a message; maybe it is preparing you for what you will do next."

This wasn't what I wanted to hear. It took a year before I was willing to accept that I needed to move on, but even then, I had no idea what I would do if I didn't do what I'd been doing. If my soul was telling me I was ready for something else, why wasn't it also telling me what the "something else" was? So I continued to run in place, hoping to be inspired with a vision of what my next move should be. The message came, but not at all in the form that I expected.

It was a time of turmoil in the organization. Rumors alluded to a major rift among key members of the management team, and employees were informally picking sides, jockeying for position in a race they each hoped would go their way. All of us working in our division comforted ourselves that our leader occupied the power corner and would surely prove victorious. As a top manager in his organization, I told myself I wasn't worried.

In the midst of this sour stew, I was summoned to the president's corner office, where he informed me that he was leaving the company. I was dumbfounded and feared what this might mean for me. He confirmed, "You are one of my key managers, and I want to take care of my people before I go. I'm making some career moves for you and others." I couldn't imagine what he had in mind, but I hoped it would mean a more significant role for me. The room was awash in sunlight so bright I could see the dust particles floating in the air.

First, he explained that my immediate boss of nine years, a talented man who had mentored me, would be moving to a sales management position in Atlanta. Still reeling from that news, but silently hoping my time for a promotion had finally arrived, he continued. A peer of mine would be stepping into my boss's position, a job I had coveted and aspired to for a long time.

My heart was pounding so loudly in my ears that I could barely decipher what he was saying. I held my hands tightly in my lap, a discipline I'd imposed on myself in the belief that if my hands didn't move, I couldn't say something I'd later regret. Had he said he'd given my boss's job to someone else? I felt like someone who's being shot, but whose mind can't process the act until they actually touch the blood. He was still talking; I knew because I could see his mouth moving, the look of anticipation on his face, awaiting my reaction. He had recommended me for a lateral move to a job that I didn't want. My mind swirled with pressing questions: Doesn't he know that I don't want that job? Is he trying to force me to resign? Did he say he'd given the promotion, the one I felt I'd earned through dedication and hard work, to someone else? He had.

It was as if I had to lose the thing I wanted most in order to find the something that mattered. As a kid I had once dismantled a golf ball to see what was inside. After prying the cover off, with much difficulty, I discovered what seemed an endless length of rubber band wrapped around a small rubber ball. I had pried away the exterior and exposed the core of the golf ball. This, I realized, is what I had to do with my own soul—strip it down to its essentials, tender and vulnerable. There the answers would be.

True Grit

I learned the meaning of courage and resilience in the

year that followed my wake-up call in the boss's office. My immediate reaction to learning I'd lost the promotion scared me and would probably have frightened innocent passersby. Standing in the dark parking garage adjacent to our office building, I gave in to breathless sobs, then unleashed a fury of obscenities. I felt so betrayed that my first impulse was to walk out, taking my talents and loyalty with me. Looking back, I realize that I gave my company, my bosses, and my own ambition way too much power.

After all, I hadn't been fired. I took a day off to consider my options and get past the shock of losing something that was never really mine to start with. I returned with my head held high and a list of what I wanted from management. Rather than accepting the job the president had chosen for me, I negotiated a new role for myself, something I could get energized about—building a fledgling electronic learning team. Seeing the value of this proposal, the company allocated staff and budget for it, and I was on my way with a brand new mission. It salvaged my self-esteem, capitalized on my strengths, and allowed me to play a meaningful, though less visible, role in the organization.

My team and I accomplished a lot that year, and I was learning new things every day. I fostered relationships I wouldn't have made, developed professional and technical skills I wouldn't have acquired, and earned the respect of my colleagues for making the best of a bad situation. I had stood up for myself without playing the martyr or sinking into the "quit and stay" mode.

I'm glad I stuck around for that last difficult but gratifying year. It showed others and, more importantly, showed me what I was made of. It meant a lot when one of my associates confided how much she admired how I'd handled the disappointment, turned it into something positive, and shown "true grit." What I didn't know then was how much those lessons in courage and resilience would sustain me in my years as an entrepreneur.

Living on the Edge

When I think back to the years I worked for a corporation, I often wonder how I managed it all. I vividly recall Paul leading a training session on management skills for in-house managers. One of my self-ordained roles in those days was to vocalize the fears and misgivings of my own and other employees. Sheepishly, I confessed before the gathering that, by the end of a long workday, I felt so depleted that I went home every night to "veg" out on the sofa. It drew nervous laughter from my compatriots.

Like so many of us in corporations, we all lacked balance in our lives, and all felt guilty for admitting it. I knew a number of folks, younger than I, who had worked for the company since the day they graduated from college. Some of them had literally never developed a social life outside the office. Their coworkers were their only acquaintances.

I wasn't much better. For a while, the company had employees rate their managers on a variety of management qualities. While my ratings were generally excellent, my lowest scores were always in "life balance." Not only was I working too hard, but I was unconsciously teaching my employees that, to get ahead in the company, they should also work too hard. I realize now how I contributed to the perpetuation of this unhealthy practice.

All of this came home to roost in May of 1995. It had started out as a marvelous Florida spring day when the fuchsia oleander were bursting and the humid air hung motionless. I'd finished an early morning meeting with a staff member and headed back to my office to tackle paperwork. My office was bordered on two sides by windows from floor to ceiling. On bad days I sometimes had the sense of falling over the edge, so I placed my desk away from the windows with my back to the interior wall. Out of the blue, I began to feel a tightening in my rib cage that traveled up my neck to my jaw. I sipped some coffee and tried to get hold of myself, but I was shaky on my feet. I tried to identify the pain in my chest, but it was like nothing I'd felt before.

The colleague I'd been meeting with returned to my office to ask a question and, from the startled expression on her face, I knew I must look as badly as I felt. By this time, I was coming to believe I was having a heart attack. When she offered to drive me to the hospital, I did not resist. After several hours of tests in the emergency room, I was sent home with a prescription for antacids and a lecture on stress. Thankfully, it wasn't a heart attack, but it was all the warning I needed. Within two months I resigned, and the only thing I was working on was a tan.

Certain times in your life you can just feel the hand of the Lord at work. Those weeks before I made the decision to leave my regular job were that kind of time for me. In addition to my health scare, the wonderful nanny who had cared for my daughter since infancy had to quit for medical reasons on the day I was to leave for a ten-day trip to corporate headquarters for the annual meeting. By the grace of God I got through those stressful weeks, but the Lord couldn't have been any clearer if He'd shouted, "Get out!" All the signs were telling me it was time. Finally I was ready to grasp the next phase of my life, whatever it might bring.

Mile Markers on the Road to Entrepreneurial Enlightenment

One of the first things I did while working on my own was to attend a career and life-planning seminar developed by one of my favorite authors. The course was inspiring for two reasons—the stories the author told of life changing events he'd experienced and the open dialog among participants. However, what sticks in my mind was a brief exchange I had with a woman whose identity completely escapes me. We were discussing our situations. She was employed full time and looking for more of a challenge; I explained proudly that I had just started my own consulting business.

She asked me a simple question, "How will you sell your services?" I gave her a simpleton answer, "Oh, I'm not a salesperson!" With a puzzled look she queried, "Well then, how will you survive?" Indeed! Like many uninitiated entrepreneurs, I was only interested in doing "my work," those activities that someone used to pay me to do, because I was on the payroll. At some level I knew I would have to *get* work, but I never thought consciously about having to sell my services and myself. While my naiveté was embarrassing, I am grateful to that woman for challenging me, early on, to face the fact that doing what you're good at isn't enough. Entrepreneurs are always salespeople in addition to whatever else they do. I set about rethinking my approach to my new livelihood.

In the second year of being on my own, I had the opportunity to teach the career and life planning seminar that I had taken earlier. Facilitating the program with many different types of groups stoked my interest in the twists and turns of people's careers and fired my passion to tell my own story again and again. On one particular occasion, I trained a savvy and experienced group of facilitators to teach the life-planning program. They expressed keen interest in and support for my leap of faith from a corporate job and my subsequent entrepreneurial journey. I was humbled and gratified at their sincere curiosity and compassion, as I tried to encourage their dreams with my own tale of struggle. It became clear to me then, and clearer now, that one of the joys of entrepreneurship lies in giving back the wisdom gained.

So fired up was I about this career and life planning program that I actively sought out opportunities to sell it, so I could teach it. I took it upon myself to approach several organizations about it and landed two opportunities to pilot the program. I contacted the author and explained that, while these were not lucrative deals, the exposure would, at the very least, be good marketing. With the author's approval I presented the programs, which were very successful. I was asked to continue teaching them. This time, when I approached him, the author declined. I tried negotiating a mutually beneficial arrangement, but I had created a situation that was too far outside the customary channels for his liking. He thanked me for my efforts, but in effect, asked me to cease and desist.

Since that incident, I have found myself in similar straits—"little entrepreneur meets big system"—on more than one occasion. I've learned some worthwhile lessons. First, when confronted with a seemingly immoveable object, make a well-reasoned and heartfelt pitch. Then move on. When I was working inside a large organization, I often felt the frustration of Sisyphus pushing the rock uphill, lamenting good ideas that withered along the way because the organization wasn't ready. Living in the fresh air outside an organization makes it a lot easier to pick your battles. The entrepreneur understands that if his or her message isn't accepted one place, to quickly move to a climate that's more amenable to change.

The second lesson I finally learned was to believe in what I have to say, believe in my own experience and its value. Early on, I expended a lot of energy representing programs that were excellent, but were not my own. I finally came to understand that the only way to assert some control over the outcome was to develop my own programs. That way, success or failure would depend on my ability to offer something of value and convince people of it. It was a plan that couldn't be thwarted by other people's agendas. Had I really believed in myself sooner, I could have saved myself some trouble, but we learn our lessons when we are ready to learn them.

Like a hiker surveying the road traveled, I could see the progress I'd made step-by-step. From a naïve beginner, who thought I didn't have to sell, to a budding entrepreneur feeling my way along the path, I had learned a lot through trial and error. Before continuing my journey, I settled briefly at a plateau to reflect and regroup. It would be some time later before I would look back and see the Spirit's guidance in these early milestones.

Creating a Custom Life

To my surprise and delight, my instructional design business took off in the third year, an eighteen-month period in which I juggled five major projects and had six associates assisting with their completion. This newfound success presented a variety of challenges and opportunities. It was the first time I conceived of my venture as a business, rather than as a series of temporary freelance assignments. In the early years, wanting to keep expenses low, I fashioned homemade business cards on my computer. It seemed time to choose an appropriate business name, design a company logo, and get letterhead printed. I met with my accountant to learn more about taxes, paying contract workers and purchasing professional liability insurance.

I was enjoying the fun of building a new business and reveling in the satisfaction of earning a respectable income while maintaining my freedom. It seemed that at every turn, a new blessing came my way. Clients recommended me to others who also became clients. When I was desperate to find an associate to help with a large, new project, I got a call from a talented, former colleague who decided to take a leave of absence from teaching to help me with the project. Paul leveraged years of volunteer work with an organization into a sizeable project for the two of us to share. Times were good, and I was feeling very blessed.

However, as projects lingered on and costs piled up, I began to feel the double-edged sword in my gut. Christmas that year was a blur-- an exhausted pause in a continuously running, fast-forward movie. I had to play referee between two associates working on the same project who bickered and lamented about each other's errors and shortcomings. In scrambling to find another contractor, I hurriedly hired a woman new to the area who was referred by a friend. Mid-project, I discovered that her skills were lacking and that my client didn't like working with her. I negotiated a mutually acceptable solution that saved the contract, but I was succumbing to the same kind of business-related stress I'd only recently escaped. When things began to wind down, I did some serious re-evaluation and made the decision that I wasn't willing to make the trade-offs to grow my business into a thriving enterprise. Maintaining the life balance and peace of mind I'd worked so hard to achieve meant more to me than running a financially lucrative business.

This was no small decision. Ever since adolescence, earning the respect of those I admired, mostly my dad, and being recognized for my achievements were of utmost importance to me. As a child of the feminist revolution, I had always taken pride in being able to "make it in a man's world". My dad, a self-made and highly successful businessman, had always encouraged my siblings and me to start our own businesses. Though he died prior to my entrepreneurship days, I felt that Dad would be proud of my success in a business of my own.

However, my dad knew—as did I—that my first priority was my young daughter. As a single mother, I had taken a huge risk in trading the relative security of a corporation for the unknowns of entrepreneurship. Many sleepless nights preceded and have followed that decision. Fortunately, my mother's depression-era frugalness and resourcefulness have molded me, and we have lived well, though modestly. Somehow I felt that the dues I paid working as a corporate consultant—long hours, frequent travel, pressing deadlines—were paying off in the ability to finesse my reputation and experience into steady income.

My goal throughout this period was to support our little family while also doing work that was meaningful, challenging and innovative. After a few years on my own, I found myself in the enviable position of turning down work that didn't interest me and seeking out projects that appealed to my creativity and sense of purpose. I sought two kinds of clients—local firms, so I wouldn't have to travel away from my daughter, and non-profit organizations, so I could feel that the time I invested served a greater purpose than my own pocket. I was blessed with both.

A friend once told me she admired me for having the courage to live my life on the edge. I hadn't planned to do that, but I did become almost obsessed with the idea of creating a life that I could live on my own terms, a life that fulfilled God's purpose for me. Many times I have felt pulled in so many directions that I feel dismembered from my own soul. Many times I have felt afraid. One image has pulled me through: I am walking through a lightless forest path, with shrill shrieks and suspicious slithers surrounding me. I slowly put one foot in front of the other, groping along, feeling my way. The blackness of night obscures all signposts; my eyes are downcast. I cling to the hand of my steadfast guide. The sound of his breathing, the warmth of his palm, the sure-footed movement of his gait—these are how I know I am still alive. He sees through the darkness, through the forest and beyond;

He knows the way. I realize He *is* the way, so I keep walking, keep holding on, keep breathing.

Forward to the Past

In the sixth year of my own business, I hit a wall. My last paying contract was a misty shape in the distance. Looking forward, I saw nothing but thick fog. After six years of successes and setbacks, I was facing a murky state of uncertainty. My days melded together, unmarked by momentous events or nail-biting deadlines. I wondered if I was wandering. As I confided in a friend, "Why is it that what I'm good at, the work I've built my reputation doing, no longer excites me?" A languishing economy and my own personal choices, made for the right reasons, had caused my business to falter. Having conquered many of the entrepreneurial dragons, my interests had evolved in new directions. I needed something I could feel passionate about again and something that would afford me a more predictable source of income.

At one point I was invited to interview for a senior position with a local educational organization. I drove to the interview on a particularly steamy day and had to park my car in a remote, gravel lot adjacent to the office building. Gingerly, I made my way, in heels, on hot gravel that reminded me of those trendy, but painful, fire walks. Stopping in an alcove of the building to tidy up, I discovered that the sole of my shoe had completely disintegrated, succumbing to the sizzling rocks. I took this as a bad sign. "Soleless," I entered the interview room and tried for an hour to conceal my hapless foot from the eyes of a ten-member search committee. Ultimately, the budget ax felled this as yet unfilled position, but I later realized that the job, had I won it, would surely have exacted a high price, my autonomy and peace of mind. This wasn't the right place for me, and while my sole may have succumbed, I left with my soul intact.

I am a seeker; I am always looking for the next challenge, for the next orchard ripe with new fruit that I have never tasted. When I was seventeen, I took a driver education course from a kind, and very patient, retired teacher named Mr. Ott. He emphasized the importance of keeping my head up and my eyes out there on the road. His favorite advice to me was, "Laura, aim high." Just in case I missed his meaning, he added, "This is good advice, not just for driving, but for life." I took Mr. Ott's philosophy to heart, and I have tried to aim high in all my endeavors ever since.

Today, I am looking toward a new horizon, and yet my destination is as shrouded as Oz viewed from across a field of poppies. Curiously, I feel pulled forward, not by forces outside myself, but by a drive within. In contrast to the popular movie title, I feel I am going Forward to the Past—recapturing a part of myself that once flourished, only better, wiser. I am drawn to that girl, that me at seventeen, who hungered to visit Europe, read the great authors, live as an artist, write the great American novel, and of course, end suffering in the world. If, as William Wordsworth wrote, "The child is father of the man," then surely I, as a woman in middle age, owe much to that girl of seventeen who pledged to aim high.

If we are artists of our own lives, then I have known for some time that my present canvas is almost finished. My time as an entrepreneur may be dissolving, making way for a new beginning. I have mixed feelings, because I have loved this time, this creation I have been working on for nearly seven years. The colors of it are misty purple and pearly azure blue, like a Florida sunset when the reds and oranges have descended below the horizon. It has the restfulness of deep water and wind in the palms. I am so proud of this canvas, but I am beginning to understand that it is finished. Knowing when to stop is, after all, the real art of it.

When beginning a new piece of art, fear and excitement are all rolled up together. One misses that feeling of flow that comes when a work is well underway. A new canvas is so bare, so frightening and so full of possibilities. Did Monet wonder, each time he began a new painting, if there were enough water lilies left in him to start again? Can a middle-aged woman run out of inspiration the way she runs out of eggs? Only if she stops tending the lilies inside.

Visitors to Central Florida often marvel at our lush, semi-tropical vegetation. When you live here, you learn that nature provides a deceptively harsh climate for plants in this region. The occasional droughts drive roots deeper to find life-sustaining water. Periodic freezes wither the vegetation, but clear out the overgrowth and kill off mosquito larvae and other harmful insects. Tropical storms batter trees and plants, but replenish the underground aquifer. This give and take dance of nature, played out over the centuries, yields a hearty landscape where only the strong survive. Trees and plants with strong roots— roots that have had room to spread out and nutrients to grow deep—emerge stronger from this tango with nature. And so it is with us, when our roots are strong and deep. Beautiful as the leaves and flowers may be, what matters most for survival is what lies below the surface. For you and me what matters most, a vibrant soul life, is what the world doesn't see. Finding the right environment for growth, a place to thrive, is my ongoing challenge. Perhaps you too are seeking a greenhouse for the soul.

Reflections

- *Do you invest your work and all of its trappings with too much power over you? How can you keep the proper perspective on your career, so that you work to live, not live to work?*

- *How do you respond to career setbacks? Anger and blame? Self-recrimination? Sadness and grieving? What source of strength could you tap that enables you to push through these natural, human emotions to a deeper place of optimism and resolve?*

- *How attuned are you to the road signs, both external and internal, in your life? Are you conscious of the direction you are traveling or are you driving on automatic pilot? Do you periodically pull into a rest stop, check the map, rest your eyes and take stock of where you are in your journey? If not, resolve to do it soon.*

- *Have you found a recurring image, phrase or prayer that comforts and steadies you when times are tough? Cling to those words and images; they are your eye of the storm when the world is spinning around you.*

- *Are you consciously tending to "the lilies inside"— your soul life, the source of your inspiration? Are you feeding your roots so they reach deep below the surface and anchor your life? Resolve to pay attention to the climate in which you are living and create your own living greenhouse.*

Part Two

The Twelve Faith-Based Entrepreneurial Qualities

> *"Learn to get in touch with the silence*
> *within yourself and know that*
> *everything in life has a*
> *purpose."*
> Elizabeth Kubler-Ross

Introduction to the Twelve Faith-Based Entrepreneurial Qualities

As our friendship grew, we learned something important about each other that we have nurtured. Each of us has a strong spiritual side balanced by an equally strong practical side. Consequently, almost all of our individual and collective pursuits seek to meld the spiritual and the practical. When we began planning *Soul Business*, we knew we wanted to craft our message in such a way that it would appeal to the practical and spiritual realms. Our goal was to frame our experiences and pass along our learning to people of faith who are also levelheaded, feet-on-the ground business people. For many months we struggled with how to articulate, how to characterize, what we were feeling and experiencing as entrepreneurs. We each compiled our memoirs, our stories of cutting the apron strings with corporate America, but we couldn't put our finger on where it was leading.

Sometimes it just takes asking the right question. We began by asking ourselves: What does it take to succeed in your own business? With over forty years of combined experience in identifying skills and

49

competencies, we quickly generated a list of them—self-confidence, independence, risk-taking and so on. We knew they were important and necessary, but the list didn't go far enough. You can find countless lists of entrepreneurial skills and traits, and we have. We've reviewed many of them and weighed their merits for inclusion here. However, we felt we had something different to say, something to add to the current thinking.

What we consistently returned to was the sense that we are on, not just a career track, but a faith journey. Our faith, woven as it is among the fibers of our whole lives, is an integral part of who we are and what we do. So we reframed the question to: What are the qualities that *a person of faith* must possess to succeed in business and in life? Almost immediately we were able to get in touch with our own experience and the experience of other entrepreneurs to create the list of Twelve *Faith-Based*, Entrepreneurial Qualities presented here. They flowed forth and felt right from the beginning—simply by asking the right question. That will be enough for some of you; others will want some validation or documentation to give credence to this list.

So, we have researched other lists of entrepreneurial traits, skills, competencies, etc. They are often the same concepts as ours with different names—names that are more readily accepted in the world of business. For example the Small Business Administration identifies "the ability to accept change" as a critical success factor for entrepreneurs; we call it resilience.

A small business center in one university believes "social responsibility" is a required attribute; we call it stewardship. Many companies today view "risk taking" as a key skill for leaders; we call it by its original name, courage.

We believe our Twelve Qualities are different, because they are infused with two core beliefs. First is the conviction that God is our business partner. It is through His grace that opportunities arise; key relationships develop; inspiration flows; and obstacles shrivel. Second is our belief, resulting from years of practical business experience, in clearly defining the behaviors associated with each of the Qualities. It is not enough to say that an entrepreneur needs discipline, initiative and creativity, since those terms can be interpreted and misinterpreted in so many ways. We were determined to convey in behavioral terms what these sometimes elusive Qualities really mean in the context of business today. We wanted to give entrepreneurs, and working people generally, a framework for examining their own behavior, a set of criteria for holding themselves accountable to an independent standard.

In Part Two we have attempted to define and describe the Twelve Qualities in several ways. First, we provide illustrations, stories from our own experience that capture the spirit of each quality. Then, we offer a set of Accountability Standards, behavioral descriptions for each quality. The Accountability Standards help you answer two questions:

- How do I know when I am displaying and living by the Twelve Qualities?
- What will I see myself doing or saying that lets me know I am living up to the Twelve Qualities?

Each Quality section includes a series of Reflections, thought-provoking questions for each of us to ask ourselves, not just once but on an ongoing basis. We conclude each segment with a brief meditation or prayer about the Quality. Finally, we have sprinkled each section with inspiring quotations from a variety of people whose thoughts we felt were worth repeating.

We have used the Twelve Qualities ourselves in a variety of ways, and we encourage you to experiment and discover the ways that work best for you. The Twelve Qualities can be used to:

- Check your decision-making process when struggling with a difficult professional dilemma
- Maintain greater balance between professional and personal priorities
- Assess periodically whether your business interactions and goals are aligned with your values
- Understand more clearly where a client or colleague may be experiencing difficulty in order to lend a hand
- Counsel potential new entrepreneurs or employees who want to know what it takes to succeed
- Provide focus for daily meditation and reflection

No rules govern how you use the Twelve Qualities, but

we suggest you try meditating on one Quality each month over the course of twelve months. See if you don't discover, as we did, the power of these Qualities to reshape your thinking about how to do business as a person of faith and to focus your search for God at work in your work.

Integrity

> **"Integrity is keeping the small promises that we make to ourselves."**
> Richard Leider

What Price Integrity?
Laura's Thoughts

When I met Marty she was in her mid-fifties and recently divorced with two grown children. She had left a job as director of human resources for a large company and moved to Central Florida to be near her ailing father. Marty was a woman in transition, who had been referred to me by a mutual friend. I was glad to do what I could to help Marty out and pleased to have found a seemingly qualified person to assist me with a short-term project.

Marty and I met to discuss the work, but it seemed, in retrospect, that she was consumed with the details of her move, her father's condition, and her search for an eventual full time position. I should have realized that Marty's lack of focus on my project was a glaring yellow caution light. We agreed on what she would do and what I would pay her. We seemed to get the project off to a good start.

As the weeks dragged on, however, Marty had good intentions, but increasing difficulty keeping up the pace. I found myself spending more time planning Marty's work than I had bargained for and even redoing some of it. Then, my client shared her misgivings about Marty—criticizing her writing, objecting to her style, and finally accusing her of plagiarizing portions of the booklet we were writing. I was caught between the proverbial rock and a hard place. I tried negotiating a compromise, but the client was adamant about having Marty removed from the project. While I didn't believe that she had done anything inappropriate, I too was disappointed in Marty's performance. I also knew she desperately needed the money I was paying her.

When I worked for a major consulting firm that used many contract writers, it was standard practice in a case like this to simply cut the contractor loose. It's a harsh tactic that's rarely a win-win. I know, because I've been on both sides of it. In my corporate management role, I once dismissed a contractor for, what seems now, a fairly minor infraction. When the tables turned, and I was contracting back to my former employer, I experienced first hand what's known among independent contractors as "scapegoat-ism." That is to say, when things go south on a project, a head has to roll; as the theory goes, this must happen to appease the client. It's understood that part of the contractor's role, even if he or she is not at fault, is to place his or her neck on the chopping block to satisfy the client's thirst for blood.

So, now that I have my own business, employing my own sub-contractors, I have a strong desire to resolve these situations in ways that are fair to all parties, without jeopardizing client relationships. For me, a fair resolution of the situation with Marty was a mark of integrity.

I decided to speak candidly with Marty, thank her for her contribution, and pay her about two-thirds of the agreed upon fee. She seemed relieved to be released from the project and agreed to my solution. I was able to inform my client that I would personally complete the project, which pleased her, and that I would reduce the price to compensate for any trouble that was caused her. In the end, I had to work a little harder for less, but what price can you put on integrity?

> **"May integrity and uprightness**
> **preserve me, for I wait for you."**
> Psalm 25:21

Does It Make Sense to Right-size Wisdom?
Paul's Thoughts

Some years ago, in the early 90's, while attending a holiday season party, I realized that a number of us who were approaching 50 seemed to be participating in what was becoming an annual ritual. We were discussing our companies' performance over the past year, and those of us who worked for organizations that had not experienced significant growth were questioning the stability of our jobs. We were talking about the realities of being "downsized" or "right sized", and the new uncertainties and interesting possibilities that seemed to encompass our futures. Ten years later, I've found that many of us have started our own businesses, found new jobs that we accept on challenging and personally fulfilling terms, or transitioned into new lifestyles that give us time to enjoy our families and contribute to our communities. We consider ourselves productive and happy.

In retrospect, we were amazed to admit that it had been time to move on. This realization made me wonder: What might have happened if our companies and we had recognized this period of mid-life awakening as a fact of life? What if we had proactively looked for ways to "restructure" the traditional employment contract in ways that would work to the benefit of both parties?

Depending on the state of the economic times, many companies and employees go through a counter productive annual ritual that determines who stays and who goes. Realistically speaking, I believe that most employees today know in their hearts that the viability of their current jobs will be reviewed on a yearly basis. The unstated reality is that most of today's employees are on one-year job contracts.

At some point, the honest approach would be to recognize this fact and open contract discussions to all employees who approach a designated tenure level with the company. Rather than brow beat and lay off employees, a company could offer to pay employees who desire a new employment agreement on a scale commensurate with the services that the employee was "selling" back to the former full-time employer. The hours would vary based on the needs of the employer and the needs and desires of the employee.

My experience has shown me that a growing number of baby boomers aren't emotionally or financially ready to settle for the traditional retirement package. Many of us relish the freedom to work and contribute to new companies, to our families, and to our communities. Most of us don't remember with fond memories the companies that sent us out into this brave new world via the traditional modes of downsizing/right sizing. We take these opinions and feelings into the marketplace. It's a shame that we all didn't benefit from a clearer understanding of how to creatively manage life's timing.

Accountability Standards for Integrity

You are conducting your business with **Integrity** when you:

- Develop and stick by a set of ethical standards that dictate how you will do business and interact with others.

- Understand and accept that you are personally accountable for perceptions of you and your company in your dealings with others.

- Stay true to yourself and your values in the face of criticism, trying circumstances, or skepticism from others.

- Make sure that others know where you stand on a question/issue, even if you must agree to disagree with no hard feelings.

- Address conflict honestly; admit mistakes; and unequivocally redress the grievance.

- Do what you know in your heart to be right, even when it means lower profit margins.

- Are genuine in your dealings with others by avoiding manipulation, pretense and tricks that make you seem something you're not.

- Give the other person/organization more than they expect from you.

- Rely on prayer-based decisions to act and incorporate prayer as a means to ensure a positive intent and course of action.

- Conduct yourself in such a way that you are always able to look peacefully at yourself in the mirror and at God in the hereafter.

Reflections on Integrity

- *What are the ethical standards that permeate your business and your life? How are you living up to these standards each day?*

- *When you are enticed to depart from your values in order to make a buck, what keeps you in line?*

- *How do you deal with conflict or misunderstandings in a way that your values remain intact?*

- *How are you consciously building your reputation so that it reflects your personal integrity?*

A Meditation on Integrity

Divine Spirit, give me the grace to be true to myself and to Your spirit within me. In the face of temptation, criticism, and skepticism help me to maintain my values and my commitments. Help me to remember that what I do defines who I am and reflects Your presence in my life.

Purpose

> *"Your work is to discover your work*
> *and then with all your heart*
> *to give yourself to it."*
> Buddha

Head, Hands, Heart
Laura's Thoughts

It took me over a year to find the right words to name my company and express the purpose for my business. When I settled on *3-D Learning,* I knew it captured the essence of my purpose—helping others learn in creative ways. What my business *does* is "Design, Development and Delivery of Learning Tools and Resources." On the surface "3-D" represents those three D words, but the name has a deeper significance, something I like to explain to my clients. 3-D also stands for three dimensions of learning that I believe must be addressed in any sound and engaging learning experience. As I explain it, learning must involve Head, Hands and Heart. In education-speak that's the cognitive, psychomotor and affective parts of the individual.

Very simply, it is a holistic approach to learning that invites all parts of a person—mind, body and emotions—to participate in the learning experience. In fact, I believe this is not so much a formula for how we *should* learn, as it is a statement of fact about how we *do* learn. As an educator and lifelong learner, I have seen the difference that learning can make in the lives of others, enabling them to grow from incompetence to conscious mastery to inspiration. The sense of purpose I feel is palpable.

But what if your job is to sell cars, repair appliances or install cable? How do you link your personal purpose with the work you do? Recently I spoke about this with a friend, Kathy, who is a stockbroker and doing quite well financially in this economy, despite market fluctuations. To her credit, she takes a very humanistic approach to financial advising. She sees herself as helping her clients secure their futures by funding their retirement or their children's education. Kathy feels so blessed by the monetary rewards associated with her business that she tithes at her church (That's ten per cent off the top.) and gives a week of her time each year to repair buildings at a rural camp for troubled youth. In the fast-paced, often brutal world of stockbrokers, Kathy invests her time with the same sense of purpose that she uses to invest her clients' savings.

Are you investing your time with a sense of purpose? For one week, calculate how you spend your time and your energy. It will tell you a lot about what's important to you. Whatever your job may be, do it in a way that connects with your deepest values.

Recently my telephone was out of order, and the repairman arrived to troubleshoot what he assumed would be a simple fix. It turned out to be more complicated, but he showed no sign of irritation as he climbed up and down the ladder into my attic during a near 100-degree heat wave. He patiently, but not condescendingly, explained the problem to me, repaired it, and joked around with my daughter and me. I was so impressed with this man who was both efficient and competent; more importantly, he seemed to grasp the significance of his efforts and the importance of customers. It seemed to me, he has a clear sense of purpose about the work he does.

Your purpose doesn't have to be a glamorous one; providing for your family may be purpose enough. Yet having that sense of purpose does great things; it grounds you in the knowledge of why you are here and keeps you plugging along despite the day-to-day distractions. Your purpose is your charter and your marching orders.

> **"Purpose is your reason for being,
> your answer to the question,
> 'Why do I get up in the morning?'"**
> Richard Leider

Eliminating the Competition?
Paul's Thoughts

Eliminating the competition is considered a surefire method in business, but in reality it is a sure way to limit and then eliminate the purpose of *your company*. Consider just how limiting and dangerous this focus and approach may be to your company. I once worked in a situation where we spent hours trying to outfox a stalwart and fast growing competitor. I realized that we were reacting to initiatives and creative choices that the competition was presenting to our customers and prospects. Our focus on trying to eliminate the other company had diverted our attention from developing our own programs and services. We were on the defensive. The competition had, in fact, seized the day.

When you find your organization locked in a highly competitive situation, why not refocus on better ways to serve your customers and improve your own products, programs, and services? Why not look for new initiatives that build your company and offer opportunities for your own employees? That's a more worthy purpose than eliminating jobs, incomes, and career opportunities for other people. Wasting precious time and focusing on a negative mission can ruin your company...quickly.

Being aware of your competition can help sharpen your company's purpose. Competition is a sure indicator that there is a market for your company's products, programs, and services. Competition challenges everyone in your company to seek avenues of continuous improvement. Competition provides you with an honest measurement that reflects your company's true value in the market place.

Accountability Standards for Purpose

You are living and working with **Purpose** when you:

- Search your soul to discover God's purpose for your life, and once found, write it down where you can see it daily.

- Are clear about what you are trying to provide your clientele and why it has value to the client and to God.

- Seek out work that is compatible with your purpose and reject work that runs counter to your purpose.

- Ask continually the question, "Where does God fit here? Is this endeavor an example of the best use of my time, talents, and financial resources?"

- Use a statement of purpose to critically evaluate your work performance.

- Evaluate periodically whether your products, services and operations are still on purpose and realign your efforts with your purpose, as needed.

- Bring a sense of purpose to the most mundane, repetitive and unchallenging tasks you must perform, knowing that these basic tasks are made holy by a higher purpose.

- Are willing to give control over to God and to respond when God calls you in a new direction or to a new mission.

Reflections on Purpose

- *What is the competition telling you about the strength of your company and the value of what you do?*

- *How is your purpose reflected in the products and services you offer your customers?*

- *Does your business purpose also serve your personal goals and values?*

- *When was the last time you reevaluated your purpose to determine how well it fits with who you are today?*

A Meditation on Purpose

God of Wisdom, help me to discover my purpose in life, my reason for being. Help me to live into this purpose each day, despite demands and distractions that threaten to divert my attention. Help me to value even the most mundane tasks when they are done in service to You.

Paul Bruno and Laura Capp

Trust

> *"Just trust yourself,
> then you will know how to
> live."*
> Goethe

Noah and the Bone
Paul's Thoughts

My wife and I were in our family room reading when Noah, our golden retriever, who had been chewing on a rawhide bone, suddenly got up and went to Susie. My wife immediately reached into his mouth and extracted a piece of this *"treat"* that had become lodged in his esophagus. Noah, for his part, has repaid the favor with non-judgmental, unconditional, and unending love for his "mother."

Anyone who has owned pets knows that this ownership is a commitment. You follow a routine of feeding, exercising, and caring for the animal, which establishes trust. The animal responds by providing you with good companionship. The process takes work by both parties. I was reflecting on this simple act of trust between Susie and Noah, and it got me thinking about the trust issues I often observe in the workplace. Noah, knowing from years of experience that Susie has his best interest at heart, trusts Susie

71

completely. What if trust was at the core of business relationships?

I have always believed that managers and business owners must **earn the right** to manage. I find that today's employees are more talented than ever before, and they want to buy into their organization's future. They will invest their knowledge, skills, and interests in contributing outstanding performance to their companies when they believe that they are considered *significant members* of a team and when they see their managers working just as hard on their side of the employment relationship.

Successful managers make a point of getting to know their team members and take a genuine interest in them. Talented managers are clear about what they expect, and they work hard to ensure that their employees have the resources that enable them to achieve their goals. Hardworking managers are visible and engaged; they view their success as the success of their employees. Because they have taken the time to find out what is going on, good managers are able to accurately evaluate employees' performance, and they have earned the right to do so. Managers succeed by establishing credibility with their employees, by investing quality time with them, and by earning their trust.

> *"Do not put your trust in princes, in mortals, in whom there is no help."*
> Psalms 146:3

Turning Over the Wheel
Laura's Thoughts

Turning your life over to God is tricky business. Self-delusion is so tempting. For example, I'm trusting God to see that my bills get paid while I write this book. Because I believe it's what He wants me to do right now, I have curtailed marketing efforts and accepted only enough regular work to get by. What if Paul and I are wrong about God wanting us to write this book? Couldn't we be fooling ourselves out of pride or frustration with our regular business? Go with the doubter in me here for a moment. What if the economic times have slowed our businesses, and we're just "filling in" with the notion we could be writers? What if the lessons we have to teach no one wants to learn or everyone already knows? I can get myself into a real funk thinking this way, ruminating on my own shortcomings.

So, in a way, it's easier to live in this limbo of hopeful authorship than to face the possibility of my own failure. That's when I start to suspect that self-delusion is a comfortable state. After all, doing God's work is a noble calling. At dinner parties, it sounds a lot better to boast, "I'm writing a book," than to admit my business may be drying up. Am I perpetuating a delusion, even in the face of delinquent bills and broken appliances I can't afford to have repaired? See how complicated this trust issue is? Stand with me on the edge of the Pit of Doubt and experience the sensation of falling in, tumbling down, being sucked into an endless tunnel of darkness. That's my fear place which keeps me, certain that my soul train is plunging into oblivion, awake at night.

That's why I've chosen Trust—pure self-preservation. I choose to believe I have a purpose to fulfill and a mission to accomplish. I trust that this book is part of that. I trust that people and events come into our lives when we need them. I trust that the Almighty will look after me in the worldly ways, so that I may further His heavenly work. So far, I have not been disappointed.

I tend to be a high control person in the sense of wanting to be in charge of my life. For me to recognize that I'm not in charge, to willingly turn over the steering wheel to the Big Chauffeur—well that takes a large dose of trust. It doesn't mean I can be lazy or stupid or nonchalant; I still do a little backseat driving, after all. It just means that driving is more than operating the vehicle and reading a map. On this trip, only He knows the destination.

Accountability Standards for Trust

You are operating with **Trust** when you:

- Believe that God will take care of you, provide you with what you need and be there for you during the rough times.

- Trust in yourself, your experience and your instincts; God has entrusted them to you for His work.

- Find and work with people you trust and who trust you.

- Steer clear of ill-defined and ambiguous agendas.

- Are willing to earn trust by anticipating, responding to and exceeding expectations.

- Earn the trust of others by never criticizing another person behind his/her back.

- Look for the best in others and assume, until proven differently, that their intentions are positive.

- Seek to build rather than destroy and to be known as a person with positive intentions.

Reflections on Trust

- *When was the last time you had a "heart-to-heart" talk with the Lord about His design for your life?*

- *How many people do you have in your life that you trust completely? How trustworthy have you been toward the people who are counting on you?*

- *In a work setting, what do you do to earn the trust of your employees, colleagues, and/or customers?*

- *How well do you trust your own experience and instincts and does this self-trust shape your behavior?*

A Meditation on Trust

Eternal God, help me to make time to get to know You, for it is only in establishing a relationship with You that I can grow to trust You. Help me to be genuine in my dealings with others so that I may earn their trust. In return, help me to look for the best in others and trust that their intentions are positive. And, Lord, help me to trust myself, believing that in all things I do Your work and that my best effort pleases You.

Courage

> *"Wait for the Lord;*
> *be strong, and let your*
> *heart take courage."*
> Psalms 27:14

Remembering Jessamyn
Paul's Thoughts

Over the years I've been amazed at how many people have become some of my life's *"accidental teachers."* One young woman, Jessamyn, deserves a special note. Jessamyn and her family attended our church and early on, I was distantly acquainted with her and her parents. In 1991 Jessamyn and her mother, Cynthia, were members of a missionary team that included parishioners from our family's church and participants from a variety of denominations in Central Florida. We toured cities in the former Soviet Union on a three-week evangelical mission. All of us enjoyed watching Jessamyn, a 14 year-old at the time, dive headlong into an adventure of discovery and make new friends in a country that had been dubbed as the "evil empire."

Upon her return from this trip Jessamyn proceeded into her high school years and shortly thereafter began to experience health problems that were eventually diagnosed as a rare form of cancer, Askins Tumor. She fought the disease and graduated from high school, but eventually was forced to withdraw from a normal life routine. Uncomplaining, Jessamyn entered into three and a half painful years of repeated hospital stays and chemotherapy. She lost her fight to survive and passed away in December 2000.

During the course of her illness, Jessamyn and her story became a source of inspiration to all who knew her. She made many new friends, some of whom she never met face-to-face. She became an advocate for disabled people everywhere. She maintained as much independence as possible by starting her own jewelry business and sold her artful creations to customers from her hospital bed, her home, and over the Internet. Cynthia often remembers her daughter with the phrase, "She lived her life a day at a time more than anyone I've ever known."

Jessamyn was one of my "accidental teachers;" maybe you have some in your life. My hope is that you will recognize their legacy of wisdom, courage, and generosity of spirit, as I did Jessamyn's, and that it inspires you to positively cope with the challenges in your life's journey.

> *"Courage is the price that Life extracts*
> *for granting peace."*
> Amelia Earhart

Reluctant Inspiration
Laura's Thoughts

Unlike the other Qualities in this book, courage is an unplanned virtue. While purpose, discipline and generosity require intention and forethought, no one sets out to be courageous. We are called to courage through life's circumstances. Most of us secretly hope it will never be demanded of us. Yet, life being what it is, most of us will find ourselves needing to step up in some way, our mettle tested.

For some of us, our act of bravery will be performed as a matter of course, the decision having been made long ago in the deep recesses of our souls—to rescue an accident victim, to shield a fellow soldier, to minister to a dying parent. For others, courage is born out of an unquenchable thirst for adventure, risk or knowledge. Whatever the impetus, a life lacking courage is a bland existence indeed.

My daughter often teases me because I do not usually cry about sad events. Acts of courage or self-sacrifice, on the other hand, will always cause me to well up. I am moved, not so much by extraordinary demonstrations of heroism, but by quiet, unsung acts of courage that populate our lives at every turn, if we take the time to look.

The next time you see a first generation immigrant managing a convenience store, dry cleaner, or deli, ask the person to tell you the story of how he or she got there. Be prepared to hear a story of bravery. When you see a person with a physical or mental disability working in a store, factory or office, inquire about the challenges he or she faces every day just to show up at work. It will surely be a tale of courage.

I think of my friend, Catherine—mother of teenage twins, business owner, and speech/language therapist. When her father, who suffered for years with multiple sclerosis, finally had to be moved to a nursing home, she invited her ailing mother to move in with her family. In the midst of running her growing business, managing her active family, and caring for her declining parents, Catherine was diagnosed with breast cancer. Following her surgery and preparing for chemotherapy treatments, Catherine lost her father, and her mother's cancer reappeared.

Catherine will tell you that prayer, a supportive husband, and friendship got her through the worst year of her life, but I'm still chalking it up to her courage. A year later, Catherine is cancer-free and her mother is well and living independently. Catherine's speech and language business is booming, and she just expanded to a larger office space. Catherine didn't set out to be a hero. Life called, and she stepped up—with grace and courage—becoming a reluctant inspiration for all of us who love her.

Most of us see these acts of personal courage and think we could never measure up, never succeed at these "extreme games" in life that are fate's twisted turns. Yet, people do everyday, and we can too. We have private reserves of courage stored away in the cellars of our souls, and we can tap them if we will only ask the Great Winemaker for the key.

Accountability Standards for Courage

You are behaving with **Courage** when you:

- Make an honest evaluation of yourself and your relationship to God.

-

- Define a faith-based purpose for your life that provides a moral compass for all decisions and actions.

-

- Do the right thing, even when it is the hard thing, and irrespective of the worldly or economic consequences.

-

- Stand up for your beliefs; state an unpopular or unexpected opinion, and tell people what they need to hear, even if it's not what they want to hear.

-

- Are willing to share with others God's central role in the successes and direction of your business.

-

- Strive to develop and nurture the ability to say, "I am sorry. I made a mistake."—and then learn from the situation.

-

- Seek God's wisdom and have the courage to listen to His counsel.

-

- Are willing to take risks—in business and in life— that lead to growth and make the world a better place.

Reflections on Courage

- *When in your life have you been called upon to be courageous? What helped you summon up the spirit to meet this challenge?*

- *In your business and professional life, what opportunities confront you that demand courageous action? Have you stepped up or retreated? How can you respond more courageously next time?*

- *How comfortable are you taking risks? When is a risk worth taking? What do you risk by not acting? What would you do if you had the courage to do it?*

- *What blessing will you ask of God to help you be ready to act with courage when called upon to do so?*

A Meditation on Courage

Almighty God, give me the courage to cope with the twists and turns of life without losing faith. Help me to do the right thing, irrespective of the consequences or cost. Help me to be brave in the face of criticism or catastrophe. In work and in life, give me the courage to take risks that lead to growth and glorify Your holy name.

Discipline

> **"Perhaps too much of
> everything
> is as bad as too little."**
> Edna Ferber

The Secret Family Recipe
Laura's Thoughts

Years ago, when I was living and working in Chicago, I got into a discussion about the Ten Commandments with a very intellectual and spiritual fellow I knew there. He explained his belief that the Commandments are not really a set of rules imposed by God for people to follow. Rather, they are a gift from God intended to enlighten people about the way to live in order to be happy as humans. My friend compared the Commandments to the laws of nature, such as gravity or centrifugal force. Gravity isn't a rule you are required to follow; it is a principle of how nature works. Likewise, honoring your parents and respecting others' property are principles of how humans work. If we all follow them, we live in harmony.

In those days I hadn't given much thought to the Ten Commandments. I had memorized my Baltimore catechism as a child and could recite the Commandments by rote. In other words, I had swallowed them whole without ever really digesting them. My friend's beliefs gave me food for thought, and I came to value and adopt his point of view. In fact, I recognized that in the Commandments, God gave us the "secret family recipe" for how to live, thrive and find contentment.

However, the big difference between the laws of nature and God's laws is free will. We can't choose to defy gravity, but we can choose whether to live by the Commandments. That's where discipline comes in; it is the conscious decision to delay gratification, to curb one's appetites. Many of us from the "'60's Generation" viewed discipline as the ultimate killjoy. As we've matured, we've begun to recognize discipline as a path to contentment. Discipline is knowing when enough is enough; it's following through on commitments; it's having less and being more.

For an entrepreneur, discipline is not only a key to success, but an essential ingredient. The dough won't rise without it, if you will. It takes discipline to keep yourself motivated, especially if you are a one-person show. It takes discipline to make cold calls, network and generally put yourself "out there." It takes discipline to roll with the ups and downs of cash flow.

The media and trade journals are filled with stories of

successful entrepreneurs who had better ideas and turned them into fortunes. I salute them, but most of the entrepreneurs I know, including myself, are just happy to pay their bills, afford a vacation once a year, and God willing, put a little away for retirement. If your goal is to strike it rich or live on easy street, don't become an entrepreneur. Maybe one percent achieve that kind of success. If you are a disciplined and focused person who can work hard, live with ambiguity and wait for the rewards, well then you've got the secret family recipe for success.

> **"Therefore lift your drooping hands and strengthen your weak knees,
> and make straight paths for your feet, so that what is lame
> may not be put out of joint, but rather be healed."**
> Hebrews 12:12

Conscious Integrity: Obeying the Personal Disciplines
Paul's Thoughts

Over the years, I've come to believe that everyone who embarks on a spiritual journey experiences sobering moments of personal truth and awareness. When I worked in a corporate setting, it was easy to focus on other people and circumstances as key influencers of my successes. My life was, for the most part, predictable and comfortable.

Then God stepped in and "laid me off." Using a football analogy that comes from a book entitled *Half-Time,* God made it very clear that the first half was over for me, and that the second half was going to be different. Some of the plays in the first half had worked, and we were going to continue running those in the second half until we were stopped. In other areas of my life, I was going to have to make adjustments.

The timing for these realizations didn't come in an

instant. Over the first three years of being on my own, the theme of personal reassessment just became part of my business planning process. There are four disciplines that have been worked into my life, and they are currently fortifying me as I approach each day.

1. There is to be no alcohol consumption on an evening before a workday. Wine is out and water is in. On Friday and Saturday evenings the limit is two glasses of wine...period. This routine has proved tougher than I imagined. I'm thankful for the discipline.

2. Consider a month a failure only if you can't pinpoint an act of volunteer service to another organization. There is always time to serve and learn from others.

3. Take some time on Friday afternoon and review your week. No matter how difficult your week may have been, I believe that you'll still find positive accomplishments that brighten your perspective and cause you to be grateful.

4. Turn off the TV and read. Experience silence. Develop your own thoughts. Become interesting.

For anyone who is contemplating "going out on his or her own," you need to understand that entrepreneurship is a *lonely business*. You are accepting the personal accountability for the success of your enterprise, while ensuring the financial and emotional well being of yourself and your loved ones. Prepare yourself to be second-guessed and criticized— and if you experience some success, to be envied.

Accountability Standards for Discipline

You are practicing **Discipline** in your life when you:

- Begin and end each day with faith-based meditation or prayer.

- Consciously eliminate the behaviors or temptations that distract you from living into the purpose for your life and your business.

- Approach each day with a goal and move toward that goal irrespective of your mood or your physical state.
-
- Develop the ability to persevere despite obstacles, fatigue and doubts.

- Follow through on a commitment, a plan or a process even when the outcome is unclear.

- Examine periodically your results and methods and respond appropriately.

- Read and study in order to add value to your efforts and your results.

- Embrace the humility to see your limitations and let it spur you on to self-development.

Reflections on Discipline

- *What are your personal excesses that are holding you back or diminishing your performance and contentment?*

- *When you examine the state of your finances, what do you discover about your practice of discipline?*

- *Are you satisfied with the example you are setting for your family members and your employees regarding the practice of discipline?*

- *What actions and checkpoints can you put in place that will encourage you to live a life of conscious integrity?*

A Meditation on Discipline

God of Mercy, help me to accept what I cannot understand, and to stay the course despite my fears and frustrations. Give me the humility to accept that Your way is straight and true, even when it thwarts my plans. Give me the strength to cultivate contentment, a stepping-stone to Your joy.

Initiative

> **"How wonderful it is that nobody need wait a single moment before starting to improve the world."**
> Anne Frank

Time Is of the Essence
Paul's Thoughts

Some of you, like me, are endless "to do" list makers. At times we all have had the experience of creating a new list and wondering why we were "carrying over" so many items from our previous lists. We mused at how busy we had been, and yet our focus had consistently shifted to seemingly new priorities. We vowed to do better this time, but in the end, we replicated this same scene again and again.

I've become concerned for people who allow outside forces to set their agendas. I find that these apparently goal-oriented, stable people are letting other influences control their beliefs about themselves and the tempo of their lives. They are obsessed with working for the right company, progressing along their personal career path, and making monetary achievements. Their homes, their cars, and their social contacts have to be *just so*. They are continually responding to their beliefs about other people's opinions of them. They use all the latest technology and gadgets to stay informed and stay ahead. They are competitive, driven—and we hail them as overachievers while we cheer them on and on.

I was one of these "lucky" people. One day I attended a time management—a *life management*—seminar to find out why I wasn't achieving more, why I wasn't doing more with my life. I got a startling answer. We had been instructed to bring our current time planning systems to the class. The instructor began by asking us to look at our calendar for the next day. First he told us to eliminate the hours in the day that had been already allocated for meetings and appointments. Then he asked us to eliminate the hours that would be spent commuting to and from our offices. He asked us to identify any administrative time, such as time spent reading, writing memos, and responding to electronic mail. Then we were instructed to block out the times that we would normally take breaks or eat lunch. Finally, he asked, "How much time do you have left tomorrow that you can schedule to work on something important to you?" My answer was *one hour*, and this was the hour that I had scheduled for lunch!

My entire day was set up to get me to work and then respond to everyone else. As I began paging forward, I discovered that my calendar was already beginning to fill as far out as three months in advance. However, the calendar's pages were devoid of notations for family vacations, birthdays, key anniversaries, or personal goals. As a matter of fact, I didn't have any goals that weren't work or career related. Work and people affiliated with work were driving my agenda based on *their* needs and aspirations.

As I stared at my calendar, I sensed that God was re-entering my life, and that He was beside me, asking me what I was doing with my life. He asked me if I really wanted to stay on this path; He was giving me a choice. It has taken me years to appreciate the power of that moment. I simply decided to step off my life's treadmill. I told God that it wasn't working, that I needed help, and that I needed to change my approach. I realized that I was opening myself up to new answers, and that my fatigue and dissatisfaction had broken me down. I was ready to listen and try something new.

The process of a new life discovery has taken years. God has presented and gifted me with people and events that have become my life's "accidental teachers." I've learned to ask the questions: "Why Me? Why Now?, Why Not?" I better understand and accept the phrase, "Thy will be done." I've learned to ask God for direction, for advice, for help, and for discernment. I've learned that His purpose supersedes my purpose and, like it or not, His purpose for my life will win out in the end. Seeking to discern God's purpose for my life and responding to this calling is where initiative begins for me. In essence, I've learned to give thanks for my life and to be more comfortable with what has been accomplished—and more importantly, what has *not* been accomplished.

I am not a mystic; I will always be a basic, down to earth guy. I still carry a planner, and I still look like I am in a hurry. What has changed over these years is what consciously goes on my calendar. Volunteer work carries the same weight as a sales presentation. Vacations are scheduled, taken, and thoroughly enjoyed. Most days start with a block of time for centering, reading, praying and an early morning jog. A section in my planner, entitled "Giving Thanks," reminds me of *who* allowed me to bring closure to a project or achieve a targeted goal.

In short, I find that I can always find time to strive to live into God's purpose for my life; that self-starting and follow-through have to be faith-based. I know that faithful people who open themselves to new insights and find themselves adrift eventually ask the question, "God, what is it that you would have me do with my life?" When they get to this point and begin experiencing the answers, they need to be willing to take the initiative and respond, "Thy will be done."

> *"The people who get on in this world
> are the people
> who get up and look for the
> circumstances they want.
> And if they can't find them, make
> them."*
> George Bernard Shaw

Make a START
Laura's Thoughts

The first program that Paul and I worked on together w.
called *Make a START*. Originally, we developed it as a
organizational performance improvement process for a maj
company. Since then, we have adapted the process f
individual performance improvement and other uses. Wh
we see again and again is how hard it is for people to "make
start," to step outside conventional boundaries and take t
initiative.

So many business people and their employees suffer from
paralyzing malaise and cynicism. Their idealism, if they ev
had any, has long ago been sacrificed on the altar
"productivity." Some companies have even bastardized t
very notion of performance improvement by using it as
means to prune dead wood. No wonder people are skeptic
and unwilling to risk making things better for fear of reprisa
Often I hear managers decry employees' unwillingness to tal
a risk, make a stand, reach a decision or take spontaneo
action. And yet, most managers neither encourage employee
to take risks nor protect them when they try and fail.

Curiously, those who are willing to take the initiative often do so by jumping ship and catching the next boat to the port of small business. While entrepreneurship is by no means a safe harbor, it does give you the opportunity to sink or swim on your own merits. I have known several former colleagues who have blossomed on their own, freed from corporate anchors.

The basic lesson of *Make a START* is to start small, to pick an annoying, day-to-day problem or procedure that is a recurring obstacle to getting things done or satisfying customers. The *START* process is also simple; it encourages *action* by individuals or small groups. In a nutshell, the *START* steps are these.

1. **S**cope the Issue
   What's the risk of doing nothing?
   What are the potential gains by acting?
   All things considered, is it worth doing?
2. **T**riage
3. Separate the quick fixes from the complex problems.
   Focus on issues that are relatively easy to fix, but yield high impact.
4. **A**dvise Others
   Determine who is impacted by the problem and who has influence over it.
   Talk to those people and solicit their help and/or support.
5. **R**ally Resources
   Determine if you have the ability and

resources to tackle the issue.
If so, act. If not, go after what you need.

6. **T**rack Results
   How will you know you're successful?
   Decide how to set up a "before" and "after"
   picture.
   Gather the information you need to prove
   you accomplished the goal.

The idea here is *not* to get hung up on the process, a common barrier to progress, but simply to take the initiative to try, to make a start, to believe you can make a difference. Let's look at a simple example. Let's suppose that the recurring obstacle for you is your lack of a filing or tracking system for your tax-related information, like receipts, pay stubs, etc.

What's the risk of doing nothing? You feel anxiety starting to build in February and by mid-April you are in a state of panic. There's also the real possibility of forgetting something important or losing out on a legitimate deduction, to name just two risks. What's the potential gain? You restore a sense of order to your life and peace of mind to yourself, to say nothing of the tax savings from those potential deductions. Is it worth doing? Yes!

Now comes the hard part—finding a *simple* solution that you can muster the energy to put into action. In the tax example, you could take the complex approach, which would be researching, buying and learning to use a sophisticated piece of tax planning software. Then you would have to spend hours entering all the relevant information. For most of us, our eyes glaze over at the thought of it. The quick way to make a start is to buy an expanding file, make a few labels for obvious categories and simply drop receipts, etc. in the appropriate section at the end of each week. Keep in mind that there's no need to over-engineer the solution; you'll get discouraged and give up because it's too hard.

By all means involve your spouse, older children or others who have a stake in the outcome. Give them the opportunity (and responsibility) to be part of the solution. Rallying resources might be as simple as dropping by the local office supply store and buying an expanding file. Don't forget that your time is also a resource, so set aside a couple of hours to make a start. Finally, decide how to measure success. Maybe you complete your tax forms in four hours instead of forty. Maybe you avoid a tax penalty. Maybe you take your special someone out for dinner on April 15, rather than sitting in line at the post office at 11:30 p.m.

Whatever your recurring obstacle may be, resolve to make a start toward removing it. Whether it's a big thing or small, the sense of empowerment and accomplishment that awaits you when you make a *start* is well worth the effort.

Accountability Standards for Initiative

You are demonstrating **Initiative** when you:

- Accept full accountability for all your behaviors, actions, statements and performance.

- Take ownership of your time and talent by consciously choosing to use them in constructive ways that fulfill your purpose.

- Stretch yourself outside of your comfort zone.

- Explore new paths that open for you and listen for the lessons that come your way.

- Act on your personal desire to make a positive difference in the world.

- Overcome fear, doubt and confusion in order to make a start.

- Act for good, even when circumstances and outcomes are uncertain.

- Stay the course when you are convinced that you are on the right track, God's track.

Reflections on Initiative

- *When was the last time you analyzed the way you spend each day? What do your choices about time say about your priorities?*

- *How often do you let inertia, fear or skepticism prevent you from trying to achieve something you want? What is one small step you could take today?*

- *Do you have a tendency to "over-engineer" solutions whose complexity gives you an excuse to give up? How can you find the patience and humility to let go of the desire for perfection and be content with small successes?*

- *Are you afraid to move out of your comfort zone, to take a risk? How can you develop the faith that allows you to take a leap into something new, knowing God will find a way to catch you?*

A Meditation on Initiative

God of Action, give me the faith to take risks to improve my life. Help me ward off the distractions and negative thinking that keep me trapped in a way of life that serves neither my own goals nor Yours. Help me to take action for good, knowing that You value my well meaning attempts more than lofty intentions.

Creativity

> **"I saw the angel in the marble and I chiseled until I set it free."**
> Michelangelo

Envisioning Success:
Paul's Thoughts

I resent the "talking heads." I resent experts filling in all the blanks with their exquisite insights. I resent being told what to think. On the other hand, I marvel at the continuous advances in medicine and the forays that push the frontiers of outer space. I love stories of individuals, like Bill Gates, who combine an idea and passion to create companies that impact people and societies all over the world.

We are a creation of God, and we live in God's creation; so why do we let ourselves become convinced that someone else will think of the next brilliant idea? Who is at the root of that little voice we often hear telling us, "That's impossible"?

When I am working with my clients, and we find ourselves on the front end of a project, I like to ask this question: "What will it look and feel like when you have completed this project and you are totally successful?" What amazes me is how quickly people will work to minimize the picture of their success. I often hear phrases such as, "That will never happen," or simply, "That won't work."

I've learned that envisioning and feeling outstanding performance is disciplined work and, for most adults, it's not normal behavior. Where did our childhood optimism go? What happened to our imaginations? Why might it take a personal crisis to rediscover our zest for life? We need to lighten up and rediscover the fun, the beauty and the boundless potential in our own lives.

When Laura and I decided to try self-employment we immediately became more in tune with new career, work, and life possibilities that would come our way each day. We found that intriguing new ideas seemed to come to us at the oddest times and in a variety of different settings. Two serious, "middle aged," and goal-oriented people have experienced the process and feeling of creativity!

Gloriously, we've discovered that in staff meetings of one, the naysayers aren't there to critique our ideas or caution us against taking the time to explore a new concept. We've discovered a new and creative freedom to listen to what our hearts or God may be telling us to do. We've gone back to discerning our instincts and feeling our lives.

> *"Learn the craft of knowing how to open your heart and to turn on your creativity.*
> *There's a light inside of you."*
> Judith Jameson

Opening the Creative Channel
Laura's Thoughts

Several years ago, I was blessed with a pair of clients, Paulette and Cathy, who have been inspiring and enthusiastic partners. What they offered me was not merely a source of income, but an opportunity to apply and hone my own creativity. These women work for a local non-profit foundation, and their mission is to serve the needs of older adults and their families. How they found me, through a chance encounter with one of my former clients, was a miracle in itself. Over the years I have come to believe that this relationship of ours was forged in heaven.

When we began the first of several projects together, I knew nothing about the field of aging and the central role it was going to play in the years to come. Paulette had the experience and vision to see that serving this population was a desperate need, and she was driven to ensure that we developed learning programs that met the need. I was delighted to be involved with such a purposeful endeavor, but I was a little worried about the fact that *I didn't know anything about this field*! Paulette reassured me that I would have lots of help, which I did, in the form of three layers of advisors and experts.

I relied on the sound instructional design and adult learning principles I knew well, and spent months reading, listening, "translating," praying and learning. Our core team met at the outset to hammer out a vision and a set of values that strengthened us throughout the process. Each time I began one of the six parts of the program, we repeated that visioning process. I leaned on the considerable experience of the core team, who never tired of my many questions and explorations. Throughout the yearlong process, they reviewed my work and provided feedback before sending it on to national experts for additional review.

What amazed me again and again was the showering of creative ideas that seemed to flow from above. I would struggle with how to communicate a concept or frame an activity, and without fail, it would be given to me. I wanted to create a program that would be engaging, meaningful, and helpful to the older adults and family members who would experience it. Naturally, I tried things that the team felt wouldn't work, but it was through this refinement of ideas that a truly wonderful product, called *As Families Grow Older,* emerged. When it was finally finished, I had the opportunity to facilitate some of the pilot sessions, so that I could see for myself the impact it had on participants.

There were days when I was tempted to run from this enormous project. In the end, I did a lot of work on my own time, because I spent up the agreed upon budget and then some. We all just wanted it to be the best it could be, and I wanted to see it through to fruition. Now, when I take the large binder down from the shelf and look it over, I am awed at what we accomplished. I know the difference it has made in the lives of many that I have met. I am proud, but also humbled to have been chosen to serve as a channel for God's inspiration.

Accountability Standards for Creativity

You are actualizing your **Creativity** when you:

- Work to leave the world a better place, thus emulating the first act of God, creation.

- Remain open to the creative process by praying, listening and offering yourself as a channel for God's inspiration.

- Use your passion and talents to make an idea into something tangible or actionable.

- Ask God how to figure it out; pray about a perplexing topic; and envision the ultimate solution.

- Respond to God's inspiration, no matter how far fetched it may seem, how it arrives or whom the messenger may be.

- Take positive action and are willing to learn as you go.

- Test your ideas with faith-based people whom you trust to give you an honest reaction.

- Are willing to see things in new ways or combine things in ways that have not been done before, resulting in new learning, new products, new approaches and new solutions.

- Stay positive and fully utilize and explore your gifts, strengths, aptitudes, interests, knowledge and skills—the tools that God has given you.

- Focus on what you perceive to be God's purpose and vision for your endeavor and are willing to support that vision by acting, by trying, by learning.

Reflections on Creativity

- *If you were convinced that you are a creative person, how might you approach your work differently?*

- *What does creativity mean in your field of study or business? How would a creative outcome benefit the world?*

- *What gets in the way of your creativity? How can you avoid, dissolve or work around the barriers and naysayers? How can you avoid being a naysayer to others?*

- *When you encounter a problem or need an innovative solution, how often do you spend quiet time just listening? How can you develop the faith to turn the problem over to God, trusting that His grace will inspire you to find the right path?*

A Meditation on Creativity

*Creator of the Universe, You have bestowed on me all
the riches of the world. May I add to the beauty of
Your world through Your creative spirit that resides
within me. Help me to be open to serving as a channel
for Your inspiration, so that the fruits of my creativity
will serve Your purposes and
enhance the lives of others.*

Gratitude

> **"*I have learned to be content in whatever circumstances I am.*"**
> Philippians: 4:11

Gratitude Glasses
Laura's Thoughts

Gratitude is a value that must be learned. Children aren't born knowing when to say, "Thank you," and I have never seen one who spontaneously wrote a thank you note to Grandma for the birthday sweater. Children must be taught that, even if they disliked Grandma's choice of gifts, they must still thank Grandma for thinking of them. When my daughter was five years old, we attended a birthday party for a friend's child. Naturally, we brought a gift for the birthday boy, but I also brought a small toy for his toddler brother. This struck my daughter as terribly unfair, since it wasn't the younger one's birthday. In her five-year-old mind, the little brother had no right to a present.

Unfortunately, some adults never graduate beyond this childish view of gratitude. None of us has a "right" to the gifts we're given, whether they're from heavenly or earthly sources. Developing a mature attitude about gratitude demands the discipline to see the cup as half full. What corrective lenses are to the visually impaired, "gratitude glasses" are to the chronically disappointed. A bright new world opens up, a world teaming with abundant riches available only to those who can see them. In fact, gratitude is such a learned response, that when it's highly developed, you see treasures at every turn. One person's desert is another's lush garden.

When I was a child, I used to love those richly painted drawings that contained "hidden" pictures. For hours I would turn them side to side, up and down, until I located every hidden tea cup, rake and bird. Maybe it was good practice for finding the "hidden" gifts in my adult life—like relationships I bemoaned losing only to realize years later how I'd been spared from making a terrible mistake. The lost relationship, the dwindling checkbook, the job layoff, the health scare—it's hard to see these as gifts when they happen. Time, if we let it, adjusts our vision like our eyes in a dark room.

Most of us have so much we walk around in an anesthetized state. If we don't have the latest model of an electronic gadget, we feel deprived. Too many of us are experts at counting our losses and scoff at the notion of blessings. For one week, one day even, try abandoning your television, microwave, car or anything else you think you can't live without. I'm betting you'll discover that less really is more.

Maybe try the game I play to knock myself out of occasional bouts of self-pity. I call it the Gratitude of the Not's. I'm grateful for *not* being born into a life of poverty and ignorance. I'm grateful for *not* having a relationship with an abusive man. I'm grateful my daughter was *not* born with a birth defect. You get the idea. Revel in the blessings you have. Oh, and don't forget to say, "Thank you."

> *"Don't pray when it rains*
> *if you don't pray*
> *when the sun*
> *shines."*
> Satchel Paige

Celebrating the Small Things
Paul's Thoughts

When I settled on self-employment as my chosen career path, I found that, in addition to being president and chief financial officer of ReFocus, Inc., I was going to have to wear an additional hat—chief morale officer. There was no one else to help me decide that I was going to take a positive approach to the upcoming day.

With all the uncertainties and pressures of trying to establish a new business, coupled with the endless supply of bad news from the sagging economy to combative world affairs to shocking announcements of institutional scandal, I've found that to survive I've had to search for the positives in my work and personal life and give thanks for these gifts.

Think about it. In today's world, how often do you see people enjoying their families, their work and each other? How often do you see people laughing at themselves? When you are in your workplace, how often do you consciously seek and find the beauty in your workday?

For some people, the beauty may be found in the elegance and creative genius of the technology, the engineering in the systems, the thinking behind the design of the processes, or the orderliness of the procedures. Others may find beauty in the quality of the products, the effective delivery of services, the company's reputation or the loyalty of the customers. There is beauty to be found in an organization's teamwork, creative potential, new market opportunities, optimism about the future, and aspirations of the employees. Celebrate them!

The week that we opened the *Re*Focus website, Susie and I celebrated this milestone with a private "screening ceremony" and a glass of champagne. From that point on, ending each week with champagne has become a *Re*Focus tradition. Amazingly, we've found that, irrespective of the week's challenges and/or setbacks, we've always been able to identify concrete reasons for moving forward on a positive note into the next week.

Our work is a gift and a charge. How often do we step back and give thanks for this place in God's overall scheme? How often do we take advantage of our circumstances and discover the beauty in our work or workplace? How often do we give thanks for the daily opportunity to engage in the discovery of our life's purpose? How often do we find God at work in our work?

Accountability Standards for Gratitude

You are living in the spirit of **Gratitude** when you:

- Acknowledge the source of your ideas, resources, successes, and revenues and give thanks for His presence in your endeavors.

- Understand and accept that all good things come from God, even those "gifts" we don't understand or appreciate at the time.

- Listen and respond to any feedback and use constructive feedback to continually improve the enterprise's potential and performance.

- Demonstrate *conscious appreciation* toward others and their gifts, even those people who help you in seemingly small or insignificant ways.

- Reflect consciously on your blessings and avoid comparing yourself and your circumstances to others.

- Honor your own good fortune by letting others know that you are grateful for your circumstances and seeking ways to share your success in service to others.

- Acknowledge and celebrate the good fortunes of others and avoid envy and pettiness when others succeed instead of you.

- Take time to reflect on and thoroughly enjoy your blessings, rather than worrying about the next sale, project or endeavor.

Reflections on Gratitude

- *Do you spend more time counting your losses than your blessings? Do you forget to be thankful for the setbacks and tragedies that have **not** happened to you? What can you do to jump-start your attitude of gratitude?*

- *When was the last time you gave thanks for your work, your coworkers, your talents, your education, and your goals? How might you treat your coworkers and customers differently if you approached them with gratitude?*

- *How often do you demonstrate conscious appreciation toward others who help you, even in small ways? What could you do to brighten the day of a support person and let him or her know how much you appreciate the help?*

- *How often do you honor your gifts and blessings by taking time to celebrate them with your loved ones? What gratitude traditions can you begin in your family or workplace?*

A Meditation on Gratitude

Generous God, Giver of all gifts, help me to recognize Your gifts in whatever form and to celebrate all that You have bestowed on me. Help me want things less and value life more. Foster in me the humility and thoughtfulness to express my gratitude to others.

Generosity

> *"Do all the good you can,*
> *by all the means you can,*
> *in all the ways you can,*
> *in all the places you can*
> *at all the times you can*
> *to all the people you can*
> *as long as ever you can."*
> John Wesley

Rich in Relationships
Paul's Thoughts

I've learned that there is more to life than collecting accomplishments and acquiring material objects and credentials. I've come to the conclusion that the most memorable and colorful threads in my life's tapestry are the textures of my relationships with people.

At this point in my life, when my business slows down after a busy period, my reaction is not to immediately go out and try to find more business. I now view this downtime *as a gift*, and a signal to check in with the key players in my life. I look to volunteer my time in a community service endeavor or seek to rekindle my relationships with my wife, our children, my parents and friends. I find that during these periods God usually has a lesson waiting for me. At the very least,

I become more cognizant of the blessed experiences and the key people that have brought richness to my life.

During the past fourteen years, I've had the unique opportunity to work with an organization at a local community college whose mission is to train individuals with disabilities on computer programming and computer-aided design. The final graduation from this program involves helping each student enter a full time job with local companies. In my years of participation with the Center's staff and students, I can honestly say that I came away from each visit feeling that the students and their courageous stories have served to uplift and teach me more than I had motivated them.

When the Center's mission changed, and my participation was no longer needed, I heard myself asking the question, "Where am I going to find a new opportunity to give something back, to participate in a positive volunteer effort?" Within minutes my phone rang, and I was asked to participate on the Board for a home for boys who have been abused, abandoned or discarded by their families. These youngsters are desperately in need of shelter, direction, and most importantly, "tough love." God heard my question about volunteerism and gave me the answer.

In retrospect, the happiest and most relevant people that I've known have always been rich in relationships. They love people and they find enjoyment in the simple events and circumstances of their own lives.

Giving what we can to others puts us in touch with the best side of ourselves. I believe that when we reach out and extend our perspectives beyond our immediate wants and needs, this act puts us in touch with God's Spirit within us. I also believe that, in order to successfully survive in today's challenging world, we need to experience that comforting feeling of consciously submitting ourselves to God's purpose for our lives.

> *"So I say to you. Ask, and it will be given you;*
> *search, and you will find;*
> *knock and the door will be opened for you."*
> Luke 11:9

An Uncommonly Good Doctor
Laura's Thoughts

A few years ago, I attended the holiday party given by our local Chamber of Commerce of which I am a member. Through the crowd of well-dressed revelers I noticed two people sitting by themselves at a table in the corner; it was my family doctor and his wife. I made my way through the merry-makers and said hello, introducing myself to his wife, whom I'd never met. My doctor is a short, portly man whose jolly face you would expect to see in a Santa Claus suit rather than in his usual scrubs. We chatted for a few minutes, but sat at different tables during the dinner and annual Chamber awards.

All through dinner, I reflected on how odd it seemed to see the doctor at this event, since he is a private person, not given to social gatherings that involve the usual small talk and "schmoozing." I soon discovered the reason for his presence; the Chamber Board had honored his medical practice as "Business of the Year." He accepted his award in his typical unassuming way and quietly slipped out of the festivities.

While I was thrilled that my doctor had received this recognition, I admit I was surprised. You see, my doctor is not so much a good businessman as he is a humanitarian. He is an "old school" physician, the kind who still makes house calls and treats the uninsured, sometimes accepting fish they've caught or clothes they've made in lieu of payment. His unadorned office, located in a rundown building across from the main fire station, is the crossroads of our community. On any given day in the waiting room, you can see farmers and firefighters, a city councilman and the Methodist minister, retirees on fixed incomes and wealthy landowners. Nearly everyone who exits is carrying a plastic grocery store bag with free prescription samples.

No one is turned away for lack of ability to pay. Every patient is treated with dignity, and no one is treated better than another, regardless of status or means. In these times when the medical community is focused on the clock and the bottom line, this small town doctor still takes the time to call his patients himself to explain test results, even if it means calling at 7:00 p.m. when patients are home from work. He puts himself out, because he doesn't want a patient to spend another sleepless night worrying about his or her condition.

What I value most about my doctor is his genuineness; he is never condescending, loves to joke around, gives you straight talk when you need to hear it and always empathizes with those who are hurting. More importantly, he seems to understand that he has been given the gift of healing for one purpose—to give it back. Perhaps he really is a good businessman after all, because he understands that generosity is at the core of good business.

Accountability Standards for Generosity

You are acting with **Generosity** when you:

- Act on a belief in God's abundance and give of your time, talents and treasure without anticipation of reward or reciprocation.

- Share the lessons learned with others and disregard who gets the credit for the contribution.

- Adjust your personal priorities in order to share your gifts and talents in dedicated service to others.

- Are faithful in donating money to other organizations and/or individuals who are in need.

- Praise and elevate other people by honoring their strengths, gifts, and contributions.

- Find the positives in a situation or person, even when they are viewed as obstacles.

- Help out a client or employee or support a community project just because it's the right thing to do.

Reflections on Generosity

- *When was the last time you gave of your professional time and talent with no expectation of reward?*

- *What organization or group could benefit from your generosity?*

- *Do you regularly contribute financially to an organization or group whose mission you believe in?*

- *When confronted with a person or situation that you perceive as an obstacle, how do you proceed in a positive manner and with a generous spirit?*

A Meditation on Generosity

Gracious Lord, thank You for the gifts You have given me along the way and the lessons You've sent that helped me learn to use the gifts wisely. Let me always be willing to extend my gifts and my time to the service of others. For it is through my hands, my head and my heart that Your work is accomplished.

Resilience

> *"Laughter is inner jogging."*
> Norman Cousins

Making Sweet Treats
Paul's Thoughts

It was my first career sales job. It had been a great month, and I was on my way to a Friday celebration with my sales manager, Tom, and my sales colleagues. There, on a street corner in Torrance, California, I saw Tom's secretary standing with Tom's Porsche's *steering wheel* in her hand. I remember thinking, "What's he up to now?" I shook my head and laughed! I couldn't wait to get to that meeting to find out what Tom had in store for us. When we asked Tom about his secretary and the steering wheel, he grinned devilishly and simply answered, "I hope she gives it back!" He moved on to the business of thanking each of us for an outstanding sales performance that month.

Tom had a unique way of blending the pressure and accountability to produce sales results with a refreshing humor that brought fun and moments of relaxation into the job. Tom's humor was upbeat, and he was always the butt of his own jokes. It seems so different from the sarcasm and bitterness I often hear today that leaves me feeling unsettled, because someone has been diminished by the moment. With Tom, you laughed at his antics and vulnerability, because he made you see yourself and realize that your own vulnerability wasn't to be feared. You just wanted to succeed when you worked for this man. I worked for Tom over 30 years ago, and I'm still humbled by the influence that his artful approach to working with people has had on my life and my career. He was the one manager that I can say motivated me to focus on the fun of achieving results. He taught me how to "bounce back."

As I was working on this story, my wife noted that she had recently read a phrase that read something like, "Laughter clears away the cobwebs from our souls." I am serious, focused, and goal-oriented by nature; oftentimes I find it difficult to "lighten up" and find the humor in life's circumstances. By God's grace and over time, I've learned to take myself much less seriously. A few years ago I found myself in a difficult work situation in which I dreaded going to the office. I remember thinking that these times were supposed to be "character building." When someone would ask me, "How's it going?" I would reply, "If this assignment is supposed to be character building, then I'm becoming quite a character!"

When was the last time that you found yourself laughing at the situation and yourself? When was the last time that you were reminded of and fully accepted your shortcomings through laughter? Who do you consider to be an artist when it comes to making "sweet treats" out of life's ordinary ingredients?

> *"If any place will not welcome you and they*
> *refuse to hear you,*
> *As you leave, shake off the dust that is on*
> *your feet*
> *As a testimony against them."*
> Mark 6:11

The Pampered Ego
Laura's Thoughts

All of our lives we're counseled to put our "best foot forward," to make a "good first impression." We have all learned lessons from the media on how to put a positive spin on even the most dismal and dire occurrences. As an entrepreneur, you are constantly called upon to sell your expertise, your track record, the benefits you will bring to the customer wise enough to select you as a provider of goods and services. Unfortunately, some of us begin to believe our own spins.

The ego is a delicate creature. It demands protection, even pampering. The ego is highly susceptible to flattery, and possesses an insatiable desire for approval. It can drug you into seeing things that aren't there and can come to blows with those that cross it. Truth is, the ego can suck the authenticity right out of you.

While we don't want to advertise it, all of us have

suffered career disappointments and losses. A layoff here, a lost promotion there—being "passed over" leaves us feeling damaged, marked as unworthy. You can hear the ego screaming for miles.

Resilience is the opposite of narcissism. Achieving resilience requires you to look in the mirror and see what's really there looking back at you. Maybe you messed up or maybe the outcome was determined by factors outside your control. Maybe you lost the game, because no one ever let you in on the rules for winning. You have to put a lid on the ego and take a long hard look at what worked in those situations, what didn't and why. Sometimes it takes years to figure it out; sometimes you'll never know, because you're missing crucial pieces of information that prevent you from understanding what went wrong. No matter. *Learn what you can from the experience and move on.*

I've never been fired from a job, but I have known the feeling of seeing the writing on the wall, choosing to resign, and hearing someone wish me luck instead of asking me to stay. Perhaps the most hurtful words I've ever heard were from a former boss, an altogether unpleasant and unscrupulous man, who accepted my resignation with glee. When I told him I had done my best for his company, but couldn't seem to please him, he retorted, "Well then, your best wasn't good enough." I still feel the twinge seventeen years later.

It takes time to recover from career losses; a certain period of grieving is required if we are to ultimately let them go and not carry the disappointments on our backs like pack mules. We must choose not to let our losses define us. We must shake the dust off our feet and move on. Oh, and we can invite our egos back for a little pampering.

Accountability Standards for Resilience

You are demonstrating **Resilience** when you:

- Turn the disappointments over to God and ask for learning.

- Bounce back from disappointments, setbacks and trials with renewed vigor and purpose.

- Accept being humbled and recognize that the disappointments are merely mid-course adjustments.

- Let go gracefully when God indicates that it's time to let go and move on.

- Adapt to changes, whether they are of your own making or not, by looking for the opportunities and lessons within them.

- Avoid losing energy by holding on to something you shouldn't or by fighting to maintain the status quo.

- Forgive those who hurt you or damage your reputation, either intentionally or unintentionally, and try to establish a continued working relationship.

- Remain in alignment with God's purpose for your life's work and stay assured that you will ultimately be successful, as God defines success.

- Seek out friends, God's cheerleaders for your life, who are willing to listen, provide loving feedback, and build your self-esteem.

- Invest energy in being a cheerleader for someone else, focusing away from your own problems.

Reflections on Resilience

- *How can you incorporate uplifting humor into your daily routines and the daily tasks of your employees or coworkers? How can you help a friend or family member recover from a career disappointment?*

- *Think about your last major career loss or business setback. How did you cope? Did you learn all you could from that situation? Were you honest with yourself and others about it?*

- *Do you have a difficult time letting go of past defeats or unexpected changes? Do you hold on to resentment, anger, shame or despair? What active steps can you take to begin the process of letting go of these negative drains on your energy and self-esteem?*

- *Do you know how to be humble without losing your self-esteem? Do you know how to build yourself up without tearing others down? What can you do to develop a fundamental win-win approach to life that inoculates you from bitterness and envy?*

A Meditation on Resilience

Merciful God, give me the strength and faith to recover from the bumps and bruises of this flawed world. Help me to see myself for what I am—imperfect and immensely valuable. Fortify me with Your love so that I may learn to take setbacks in stride and learn the lessons I need to grow.

Renewal

> *"Take rest; a field
> that has rested
> gives a beautiful
> crop."*
> Ovid

Don't Be Afraid to Sleep In
Paul's Thoughts

I'm beginning to question life's pace. We move too fast, and we're afraid of silence. The next time that you're driving your car, note the speed and how many drivers you observe using their cell phones. I am coming to believe that there is a difference between accomplishing goals and living life successfully.

During my junior year of college, I flunked an English final exam. I simply misread the essay question and regurgitated the course in my answer. I was moving too fast. When I recovered from the shock of my failure, I realized that I needed to slow down and manage my time and my days differently. I began to understand that a day is a long period of time and that working at a moderate pace and focusing on priorities still enabled me to address a variety of subjects rather well. That English final enabled me to learn a crucial life lesson. I've never forgotten that a day, a week, and a month are long periods of time, and that no matter how long my to-do lists are at the moment, there is still time to get most of the work done.

To slow down. To pace myself. To sleep in. To focus on opportunities other than the work itself. To enjoy a good walk, a high sky, the sound of my shoes while jogging, the intelligence of our golden retrievers, a bowl of ice cream, the sun coming up on an early morning run, laughter with Susie, the sunset in Key West, breakfast and lunch with close friends, volunteering and being appreciated, the wonder at life's surprises and insights.

Today we are inundated with information and modes of convenience. Hypothetically we should know more, and we should be able to do more. Do we dare break with these possibilities to slow down and let God bring our lives to us? Dare we slow down and simply sleep in?

> *"But those who wait for the Lord*
> *shall renew their strength,*
> *they shall mount up with wings like eagles,*
> *they shall run and not be weary,*
> *they shall walk and not faint."*
> Isaiah 40:31

Caring for Ourselves
Laura's Thoughts

You may have observed, as I have, that we often overlook an unmet need in society until we are personally touched by it. John Walsh's work on behalf of missing children grew out of the tragic loss of his son, Adam, at the hands of a killer. Many celebrities, whose lives have been impacted by illness or injury, have publicized their causes for the good of many. My own life was touched when I lost a friend to Alzheimer's disease; it sensitized me to the issues of aging adults and the loved ones who care for them.

Most of the assistance provided to ailing elders in this country comes from family members, whether they are spouses, adult children, grandchildren and even close friends. If ever there was a group in need of rest and renewal, it is the heroic people who serve as full time caregivers to frail elders. In less extreme ways, most of us—particularly those of us in middle age—are

141

caregivers to someone, be it children, spouses or aging relatives. Often we care for them all, in addition to holding down a paid job and maintaining a household of our own. Almost always there is no time for oneself. That reality, multiplied over the years, takes a huge toll on one's health and spirit. Caregiving is a "high risk occupation."

I will never forget the mother-daughter pair that attended one of my seminars on aging. Vi, who was in her seventies, was the full-time caregiver for her husband, who suffered from Alzheimer's disease. She was a bright and delightful person who won the hearts of her classmates with her courageous spirit that never sought pity or praise for the care she gave. Jane, the daughter, rightly insisted that her mother get out of the house occasionally and spend some time with other people in similar situations. During the weekly class sessions, we learned how dedicated Vi was and how guilty she felt for taking even a short break from her husband's constant needs. We all tried to encourage her outings and discourage her feelings of guilt about taking this brief time for herself. Vi never spoke about her own health problems, but it was not hard to see that she was exhausted. At the end of the last class, I hugged Vi and Jane good-bye and wished them well. About six months later, I noticed Vi's picture in the obituaries. Like so many older caregivers of Alzheimer's patients, she died before her beloved husband. She gave that "last full measure of devotion;" truly Vi was, like so many others, a heroine on the battlefield of Alzheimer's disease. In my heart I honor Vi, but I welcome the day when caregivers do not have to be casualties of the wars their loved ones are fighting.

Caregivers, like Vi, who cannot escape their responsibilities, need our prayers and our help for sure. However, many of us in far less demanding circumstances are also stretched too thin. It seems fair to say there is a "stress epidemic" in this country. Sometimes the crisis is of our own making—the relentless pursuit, motivated by greed or ambition, of *more*. Why not pursue contentment with the same level of determination, and let go of our self-imposed imprisonment to power, status and wealth? We may have convinced ourselves that others need this or expect that from us, but what we need for ourselves is no less significant. Renewal of mind, body and spirit is really not an option, if we want to preserve our lives—for ourselves and for those depending on us.

Accountability Standards for Renewal

You are incorporating **Renewal** into your life when you:

- Keep your life in proper balance and make time for God and loved ones.

- Allocate a portion of each day for quiet and reflective time.

- Find and develop a physical and spiritual outlet that rejuvenates you each day.

- Pay attention to the messages from your body and mind and respond by providing the rest, relaxation, or stimulation that you need to restore yourself to fullness.

- Cultivate relationships with faith-based friends and network to meet new people.

- Explore new avenues and opportunities that offer continuous new learning.

- Take breaks and vacations—put the business down.

- Take on new projects or products that challenge you, stretch you and prevent you from sinking into boredom or complacency.

- Work deliberately, seemingly slowly, to realize that a day, a month, and a year are long periods of time.

Reflections on Renewal

- *What are the little things in life that you enjoy? When did you last enjoy them? When was the last time you indulged in doing something you've always wanted to do?*

- *Do you make a practice of allocating a portion of each day for reflective time, reading of Scripture, journal writing or meditation?*

- *How good are you at monitoring your own health and wellness? How well do you listen to the messages from your body and mind?*

- *When your energy is low and your spirit flagging, how do you restore yourself to wholeness?*

A Meditation on Renewal

Heavenly Father, You have shown me the importance of renewal throughout nature. Help me to learn from Night the comfort of rest and from Winter the magic of stillness. Help me to love myself as much as You love me, so that I will care for this precious child of Yours that I am.

Stewardship

> *"Like good stewards of the*
> *manifold grace of God,*
> *serve one another with whatever*
> *gift each*
> *of you has received."*
> 1 Peter 4:10

Living in the House You've Built
Laura's Thoughts

Over the years, Paul and I have consulted with hundreds of companies on customer relations, including such topics as building relationships, winning trust, discovering needs and fostering loyalty. One of the lessons we teach is that your bond with a customer is a sacred trust. At the very least, customers deserve respect and honesty. Building long-term and repeat customer interactions takes a whole lot more. Small businesses, in particular, succeed by establishing and maintaining close relationships with customers in a specific locale or industry.

What customers want is pretty simple. They want to be treated as if you *care* about their business, and they want products and services that work the way they're supposed to at a fair price. Paul and I found a story on the Internet that we regularly share at our seminars.

No author was identified with the piece. It goes like this.

> An elderly carpenter was ready to retire. He told his employer of his plans to leave the house-building business and live a more leisurely life with his family. He would miss the paycheck, but he would get by. The employer was sorry to see his good worker go and asked if the carpenter could build just one more house as a personal favor. The carpenter agreed, but in time it was easy to see that his heart was no longer in his work. The carpenter resorted to shoddy workmanship and used inferior materials. It was an unfortunate way to end a dedicated career. When the carpenter finished his work the employer came to inspect the house. He handed the front door key to the carpenter and said, "This is your house—my gift to you." The carpenter was shocked! What a shame! If only he had known he was building his own house, he would have done it all so differently.

What you provide your customers comes back to you. If you mistreat them or provide inferior products, you will burn through customers like paper and, in time, your business will be reduced to a pile of ashes. Make every product as if you were making it for yourself.

Treat each customer as you would like to be treated. The world is full of customer relations tips, techniques, methods, procedures and scripts—many of which are helpful. In the end, though, none of it works unless you believe what the carpenter learned too late—the house you are building is your own.

> **"I must admit that I
> personally measure
> success in terms of the
> contributions
> an individual makes to her or
> his fellow human beings."**
> Margaret Mead

The New Rules for Leading Employees
Paul's Thoughts

During the past year or so, I have been conducting an informal survey of employees' expectations at a variety of companies with which I've worked. Perhaps because I am an outsider, I am perceived as more objective and safe. I have been amazed at the candor of these employee groups, who have shared their expectations with me. What I have learned are the new rules for leading employees, particularly younger employees. Here is some of what I've found.

The new employees expect interesting and challenging assignments that are offered by managers who show a sincere interest in their development. Forget the concept of "paying dues;" new employees are looking for diversity, growth, status, and purpose in their assignments. They are willing to be a cog in a big wheel, but they want to be a *significant* cog in that wheel. They don't expect to fail. They'll move on to something new rather than stay in a situation that isn't working.

The new employees are looking for a sense of excitement. They want their company to be considered a current and future leader in the field. Take time to educate them on the industry trends and your company's potential. Don't rely on senior level messages from "on high" to inspire outstanding job performance. Today's managers are expected to take more active leadership, teaching and motivational roles. Don't lecture. *Walk your talk.* They're watching you, and they size up an "empty suit" quickly.

The new employees expect to have access to the latest technology and all training and education they need to do their jobs. They want to learn, but they view blunt criticism as an indicator of failure; and failure is to be avoided at all costs. Set expectations and commit to supporting employees in their quest to be successful. Follow-through on your commitments, and ensure that the necessary training or development opportunities are delivered and linked to successful performance.

The new employees expect to be mentored. They observe and emulate versus asking questions that make them appear unknowledgeable. Help them fit into the organization. Never forget that they expect a voice in what happens to them. Partner the career progression process. If you are viewed as a partner, loyalty and outstanding performance are the potential rewards. If you are viewed as a deterrent or obstacle, employees will leave your organization at their convenience.

The new, particularly younger, employees challenge our traditional beliefs about work and demand that we rethink our approach to a highly directive management style. They are talented, smart and willing to work hard. They are seeking new role models to emulate and good organizational stewards who will shepherd them to the green pastures.

Accountability Standards for Stewardship

You are practicing good **Stewardship** when you:

- Remain mindful of the God-given purpose for your enterprise, recognizing that it is His operation and you're "managing the store."

- Let prayer guide you in the allocation of time, talents, and money.

- Set performance goals; strive to meet those goals; listen for feedback from all sources; and redirect your actions accordingly.

- Consciously make time to serve others, including your immediate family.

- Intentionally commit a portion of your earnings to needy people and organizations.

- Avoid purchasing unnecessary luxuries that you can't afford and pay off all debt.

- Hold yourself accountable for expenditures of time and resources by continuously seeking ways to improve efficiency and reduce waste or loss.

- Apply the same level of care and concern for others' resources, goals, ideas and confidential information as you would your own.

Reflections on Stewardship

- *What "seeds" have you planted with your employees and customers? Have you realized the rewards of your efforts, and if not, how can you recommit yourself to this goal?*

- *In what ways have you been a good steward of your financial, professional and personal resources? Is there more that you could do?*

- *What procedures and guidelines have you established in your business that help build trust and loyalty in your customers?*

- *Have you extended the principles of good stewardship to your family members, employees and others by letting them know what you believe and what you expect of them?*

A Meditation on Stewardship

Good Shepherd, help me to listen to my employees and my customers, so that I may understand their needs and desires, as You understand mine. Give me the humility to serve them to the best of my ability and the insight to feel honored to serve. Help me to sow the seeds that will reap a generous harvest, not for my own glory, but for Yours.

Last Thoughts

Last Thoughts: Reflections on September 11, 2001

We could not have known, when we began this book, how so many lives would change on that unforgettable day. In these pages we have shared our struggle—a struggle, not only to succeed professionally, but to find meaning in our work and to deliver on the sense of purpose we hold for our lives.

The horror of that morning, shown live on television, will never leave us. Yet, within hours of the attacks, new images began appearing on television and computer screens. We saw people, of all races and ages, reaching out and helping each other. We saw real time enactments of the Faith-Based Entrepreneurial Qualities—ordinary people having the grace and courage to take life's circumstances and meet those events head on. Courage, discipline, generosity, and resilience loomed large in this tragedy—a tribute to the Spirit of God within us that *cannot* succumb to terror, destruction or even death. God was truly at work in New York City, working through His people as they put the Faith-Based *Life* Qualities to work.

The firefighters and rescuers of "Ground Zero" in New York City captured the gratitude and awe of people everywhere, but their courage is the same courage of Jessamyn and Catherine. There is *one* Spirit of Courage, and she moves through all of us when we need her most. The conscious integrity and conscious appreciation we wrote about have shown themselves in admirable ways in the days since the disaster. Companies that have lost large numbers of employees have gained a painful and renewed appreciation of the value of their people and have demonstrated a commitment to caring for victims' families and survivors alike. From company presidents to Congressional representatives to city leaders, they are answering the call to stewardship.

In these trying times, we have seen those who chased external pleasures turn inward to ask: God, what is it that You would have me do with my life? People have begun to understand that economic wealth, freedom and even life itself are not limitless. Only love is without limits, and only love can heal. In a sobering way, this tragedy has caused each of us to examine the house we have built and to ponder how we will learn to live with the seeds we have sown. More than ever, the movers of this world have been shaken, brought to their knees in the realization that, without God, we can never turn back evil or preserve the good we have known. Perhaps even the most jaded, the most hardened are now ready to turn the wheel over to God, to trust Him to steer our course into an uncertain future.

During the national prayer service following the attacks, the Reverend Billy Graham reminded us that, as a people, we could forget the values inherent in America's foundation and, like the towers, implode on an inner core of fear and hate. Or, we could turn to God for guidance; for the courage and resolve to bring justice back into a broken world; and for the strength and patience to rebuild our cities and ourselves. How often in our lives do we reach those moments of potential and personal implosion? How often are we forced into making the decision to press on, to rebuild? How often do we look inward and wonder if we have what it takes?

Where faith and time converge, there lies hope. The fires of tragedy forge our resolve, and the tears of compassion wash us clean. We move forward, footstep-by-footstep, to a clearing in the forest. In that sacred place we gather, hand-in-hand, and move as one toward a world restored and enlightened by our painful awakenings, with souls renewed by the handprint of the Mighty One.

Soul Business's Faith-Based Entrepreneurial Qualities reach well beyond the playing field of private enterprise. Integrity, Purpose, Trust, Courage, Discipline, Initiative, Creativity, Gratitude, Generosity, Resilience, Renewal and Stewardship are the grace-filled, enabling gifts that God has woven into the purpose and plan for each of our lives. *Soul Business* is the story of two people celebrating the wonder of rediscovering God at work within our lives. We hope that our stories help you discover God at work in yours.

About the Authors

Paul Bruno and Laura Capp offer a point of view that is based on over forty years of collective experience in management, sales, consulting, human resource development and training. Paul is president of *RE*Focus, Inc., a management consulting and training company in Longwood, Florida. Formerly a successful Xerox manager, Paul also served in marketing and sales with a global training organization. Laura is president of *3-D Learning*, an instructional design and consulting firm in Oviedo, Florida. For several years Laura designed curriculum for vocational education programs and then directed the consulting practice of a global training organization. Both authors played key roles in developing and marketing selection tools and assessments for Saturn Corporation's retail automotive network, as well as other major corporations.

Paul Bruno can be reached at:pbruno@refocusinc.com

Laura Capp can be reached at:SoulBusiness4@aol.com